THE ART
OF CLIMBING

SIMON CARTER
FOREWORD BY ADAM ONDRA

229 illustrations

CONTENTS

FOREWORD
by Adam Ondra

There aren't many sports in the world that lead people to places as incredible as those encountered through climbing. Walls, cliffs, overhangs and peculiar formations can be found almost anywhere on Earth, and every rock is specific and unique, offering particular climbing. Who knew landscapes around rocks could be so diverse? Even after many years of climbing and travelling, it still makes sense to journey to new places, because you'll inevitably find something completely different and new. I am sure that photography plays an enormous role in inspiring new generations of climbers to take their first steps into the vertical world – to try an activity that might seem bizarre and pointless to many. Why climb to the top of a rock when you could simply walk to the peak from the other side?

Simon is a climber, as passionate as any I've met. His photography captures his love for the sport, showcasing why climbing is among the most awesome activities on Earth, and bringing you to many of the world's best destinations. The images in this book embody the very essence of climbing, the spirit of adventure and freedom, that will inevitably prompt readers to think about their next trip. Of course, *The Art of Climbing* reveals the best possible climbing, too. And there is no better person for the job. Simon comes from a generation of climbers for whom freedom and adventure were way more important than they are today.

Simon's shots are as diverse as climbing photos can be. They capture so many different environments – from Australian sandstone to European limestone and African granite. Simon has journeyed across the world and now, in his photography, offers us captivating views of some true wonders of nature. Through the images in this book, you can travel with him and climb with the athletes in his pictures. Let your imagination get to work, and dream.

It is important to have books like *The Art of Climbing*, especially in today's digital world. So really hold the paper pages, slow down and admire what nature has created. But also take the time to appreciate the art of capturing each image at exactly the right moment. I have spent countless hours of my life staring at climbing photos. I don't think it's made me a better climber, but it has certainly made me a more passionate climber. And often, on the climb, it is passion and spirit that actually get you to the top.

← **Let Freedom Ring (25)**
Lucas Corroto finding relief from thin crimpers on pitch four of this later-day addition at Pierce's Pass in the Blue Mountains, Australia. Pitches are 21, 25, 22, 24, 20 and 25. Jason McCarthy belaying.

INTRODUCTION
by Simon Carter

↑ Simon Carter playing with a borrowed camera on a camping trip with friends (*c.* 1983) and climbing on the walls of a suburban shopping centre in Canberra, ACT, Australia (*c.* 1985).

→ Our Terminal World (25)
Simon Carter leading, with John Fantini belaying, the first ascent of this arête at Point Perpendicular, NSW, Australia in 1992.

The Art of Climbing is a celebration of a sport that combines the majesty of nature with some of the most positive aspects of the human spirit: imagination, determination and the ability to deal with risk.

This book is also a manifestation of my childhood passions: photography and rock climbing. As a fifteen-year-old boy in the early 1980s, growing up in Canberra, Australia, I got my hands on a camera and spent countless hours experimenting. My parents helped me set up a darkroom in the laundry, covering the window with blackout cloth.

I was into the outdoors, too. My friends and I went caving, hiking and backcountry skiing. At seventeen I became fixated on mastering rock climbing and trained at every opportunity. I spent my free moments traversing the climbing wall on the outside of the school gymnasium and found buildings to climb on all over town. By the time I graduated from high school, I had the climbing bug.

My first job was in the photography department at the local university, where I spent most of my time in a tiny darkroom making prints for scientists. The work was tedious and unimaginative. After two years, I couldn't take it anymore; I quit and headed to the south of France to climb at Buoux and Verdon Gorge, then the centre of the rock-climbing universe. This two-month trip in 1987 turned out to be transformational. I returned home even more psyched about climbing, and I scored my first magazine feature with photos from the trip. I knew then that climbing photography was the ultimate combination of my passions, although the timing was not yet right to pursue it seriously.

Determined to share my love of rock climbing with others, I studied outdoor education for three years. I planned to work with children, using climbing and other activities to introduce them to the great outdoors. Climbing provides more than just an escape from our distracted material world – it gives us a connection with nature. Although my career ultimately took a different path, the importance and beauty of nature have stuck with me, and over time have become core elements of my photography.

In 1993 I moved to Mount Arapiles in western Victoria, set up my tent, and became a full-time climbing bum. On my rest days, I photographed my friends, who were some of the best climbers in Australia and were tackling super-spectacular routes. Film for my camera was expensive, so I sold images to magazines to fund my operation. This in turn inspired me to start a climbing-photography business; I now had the experience, knowledge and *reason* to do it. The timing was also fortuitous, as climbing was about to boom.

I've since had some of the best times of my life hanging off a rope or on a neat perch, taking in the majesty around me while waiting for climbers or the right light: looking through the camera, framing the shot and anticipating the action.

Getting into position and rigging ropes for a shoot can be a lot of work, just as it can be for the climbers. The effort might entail long hikes with heavy packs, climbing a route or fixing ropes, abseiling and hanging in uncomfortable positions. Scrambling around cliff tops unroped can be scary and I've become more cautious over the years. I feel best shooting while hanging off a rope I know is well anchored and not near sharp or loose rock.

Even the best-laid plans don't always work out; sometimes luck is required as well. The lighting, climber action and positioning need to all come together simultaneously. Many times I've shot the same location over and over, learning a bit each time, before I was happy with the result. Sometimes it comes down to a moment that's never again repeated, giving me just one chance to capture the magic. For the best light, I often shoot at dawn, dusk, in winter – or I might chase a certain type of cloud cover. Flirting with bad weather or a storm can enhance a shot with an added dose of atmosphere.

Rock climbers perform on nature's most spectacular stages, so I would describe my photographic style as rather 'straight'. When I've dabbled with more artistic techniques – such as closeups, blurring and artificial light – the resulting images often felt too contrived. Straight shots let the setting shine through. I strive to capture what is interesting or unique. Sometimes it's the climber or what they are doing, but often there is something about the rock, the route or the place.

Emphasizing nature has led to something unexpectedly 'artistic' consistently appearing in my work – perhaps odd, given my deliberately 'straight' style. But I have come to realize that nature does the work. My focus on uniqueness has simply allowed nature's artistry to emerge. The more incredible the natural architecture, the more beautiful the canvas, the better.

The Art of Climbing brings together a collection of my best work for the first time, capturing the apex of human pursuit and adventure in nature's most majestic playgrounds. The images, presented alongside reflections from me and other climbers, explore climbing as both a sport and an art form. Each chapter highlights a unique aspect of artistry that transpires when nature and human endeavour meet. From irresistible formations, lines and walls to the focus and intensity necessary to succeed, *The Art of Climbing* reveals the inspiration and passion that draws us to some of the most dramatic and daring reaches of planet Earth.

← Nati Dread (30)
Andy Pollitt on a hard route that he established at Mount Arapiles, Victoria, Australia, *c.* 1991.

↑↑ Anaconda (28)
Malcolm Matheson on the hard sandstone of Taipan Wall, in the Grampians, Victoria, Australia, *c.* 1993.

↑ Bard (12)
Jo Whitford making her routine morning solo of this Mount Arapiles classic, Victoria, Australia, *c.* 1991.

FORMATIONS

Extraordinary rock formations are mesmerizing; they capture the imagination of climbers, causing us to go to all sorts of effort that we might not usually. The more spectacular a formation, the greater its appeal to climbers. A truly amazing formation might inspire long hikes with heavy packs, overcoming any number of obstacles, just to make the approach. When a funky formation also provides high-quality climbing, when it's more than just a summit, it doesn't get much better.

1

Not only do extraordinary rock formations fire the imagination, but the experience of climbing one of these monoliths can also create special memories that linger on. They foster little legacies – hopefully positive ones – imprints on our brains that become part of who we are. Never has this been truer for me than my first experience with Tasmania's Tote, now nearly thirty years ago.

At first view, I knew I had to climb it. It was the most outrageous piece of rock I'd ever seen. Standing 65 metres (230 feet) high but only 4 or 5 metres (13–16.5 feet) wide at the base, and rising out of the surging ocean, this single dolerite column seemed to defy all probability: truly a freak of nature.

I was looking at the Totem Pole (aka 'The Tote') from the cliff of Cape Hauy on Tasmania's east coast. I wondered what climbers John Ewbank and Alan Kellar must have felt when they became the first people to scale it back in 1968. They had established a difficult 'aid' route up The Tote in a single day, before being forced to spend a stormy night on the summit where, as the story goes, they could feel The Tote swaying in the strong winds.

Twenty-seven years after that first ascent, I was here with climbers Simon 'Simey' Mentz, Steve Monks and Jane Wilkinson. Simey had attempted to climb The Tote several years before and his enthusiasm was infectious. I knew his dream was not only to climb it by the existing 'bash-and-dangle' aid route – where 'aiders' in the form of hooks, nuts, chains and pitons support the climber's bodyweight – but also, if possible, to establish a new route up it, a 'free' route that would use the gear only to prevent a fall. Steve was fired up too. Extremely accomplished on all sorts of rock, as well as on snow and ice, and one of best all-round climbers in Australia, I doubted The Tote could mete out much that he couldn't handle. Jane, meanwhile, had been inspired by Tasmanian adventure climbing the year before when, on a ten-day trip into the southwestern wilderness, she made the first ascent of the hardest route up Precipitous Bluff.

And me? Gazing across at this unlikely feature, the draw of its summit was obvious. I wanted to climb it for sure. But the striking aesthetics of this rock were so undeniable that I faced an internal conflict: to climb or to photograph. Could I have them both?

A short scramble down the cliff brought us to a ledge where we could gear up. A 60-metre (197-foot) abseil and a hop across some wave-washed rocks led to the base of The Tote. Steve and Simey shared the lead climbing of the aid route, while I set up my ropes and went to work with my camera.

All the fiddling with protection, hammering in pitons and trusting little sky hooks that goes with aid climbing makes it a slow

"At first view, I knew I had to climb it. It was the most outrageous piece of rock I'd ever seen. Standing 65 metres (230 feet) high but only 4 or 5 metres (13–16.5 feet) wide at the base, and rising out of the surging ocean, this single dolerite column seemed to defy all probability: truly a freak of nature."

← The Free Route (25)
The Totem Pole is an extraordinary free-standing 65m-high dolerite column at Cape Hauy on the Tasman Peninsula, Tasmania, Australia. Monique Forestier leading the second pitch to the summit, with Fred Moix belaying.

→ The Free Route (25)
Roxanne Wells on pitch two of the original free route on the Totem Pole, with Chris Peisker belaying.

process, and we had to return the following day before Steve and Simey reached the summit of The Tote. Getting off again was achieved by cleverly tensioning the abseil rope so it was strung horizontally between the summit and the starting ledge on the mainland. This design is called a Tyrolean Traverse; once it was rigged, all you had to do was clip onto the rope and slide back across the void to the mainland.

With everyone back on the starting ledge after a successful climb, Steve and Jane started the hike back to camp. It had been a tiring couple of days: cold, windy and stressful. Before dismantling the Tyrolean Traverse, I hung around and chatted with Simey. As much as we wanted to return to camp with the others, it was clear that – with the Tyrolean rope still in place – this was probably Simey's only chance to assess The Tote's potential for a free route. So he slithered back across and abseiled down its far, unseen side to check out the possibilities. Simey hardly had to say 'it goes' when he returned a while later – his smile said it all. It would be hard, but not too hard. We were going to have some fun.

The next day we headed to Hobart, hired a metal dinghy and towed it back to camp – it would transport our bolting gear to The Tote. Our plan worked well until we had to find somewhere to land the boat. Unloading ourselves and the gear was stressful; even though the swell was relatively flat, the dinghy was tossed up and down, and the potential to smash into the cliff and capsize seemed immense. We were fortunate to get away with it – with a bit more seafaring experience, we probably wouldn't have even tried it.

Steve and Simey crossed the Tyrolean Traverse to The Tote's summit, abseiled down and went to work bolting the new climb. The first pitch was an extraordinary route that spiralled around the pole, climbing on three sides before finishing on the far side, on a perfect ledge after 25 metres (82 feet) of gain. The second blasted to the top, with 40 metres (130 feet) of dolerite face and arête climbing.

The following day – that of the free-route attempt – was cold and cloudy, with a steady wind funnelling through the gap between The Tote and the mainland. The climb started from a boulder barely above water level, where the chances of staying dry were slim; tactics to keep warm would be required. Jane volunteered to belay so the others could stay warm and dry. Then, just as Steve started climbing, a massive wave came in from out of the blue. The start was now wet, Jane was soaked and the ocean looked angry. Steve wouldn't have the luxury of multiple shots at this first pitch. The pressure was on.

The climbing looked hard and blank. Steve put in a huge fight. He tenaciously figured out the crux moves and then traversed out of sight to the pillar's dark side. Eventually, Steve reappeared to us, popping his head around the corner, standing on the halfway

"Unloading ourselves and the gear was stressful; even though the swell was relatively flat, the dinghy was tossed up and down, and the potential to smash into the cliff and capsize seemed immense."

↖ Tyrolean Traverse
Having earlier climbed the existing 'aid' route, Simon Mentz uses the Tyrolean Traverse to regain the summit of the Totem Pole, so that he can abseil down to assess the free-climbing possibilities.

← Boom!
Not a great start. The moment that Steve Monks started his free-route attempt on the Totem Pole, his belayer, Jane Wilkinson, is drenched by a wave. Steve luckily stayed dry and could continue.

ledge. He let out a whelp of joy, victorious. It was a real relief: it no longer mattered what the ocean would throw at us.

The second pitch was also far from a foregone conclusion. The climbing was still tenuous and tricky. When Simey expertly reached the top, I travelled across the Tyrolean again to take some summit pictures. After the others had followed the pitch, not wanting to miss out entirely, I abseiled down and got a top rope up the second pitch myself. Now I understood what they were raving about! The climbing was superb. It would have been exceptional on any cliff, but add in the location, the journey to get here and the feeling of reaching the summit of a most extraordinary formation, and we knew this was something else. The ride back in the dinghy that afternoon was a good one.

All that remained was to persuade Simey and Steve to return the next day, yet again, so that we could get some photos with sunlight on The Tote. Back then, shooting film, I was concerned about how the pictures would come out with the heavy cloud we'd had. But once I'd got my shots, our Tote mission was finally complete. I've spent another twenty or so days out at The Tote since then, climbing, photographing and filming, but those first days remain some of the best.

I'm convinced that for climbers, time spent grappling with and playing on unusual formations is well spent. Rock formations can be truly remarkable. As climbers, we are incredibly lucky to have access to some of the most fantastic playthings in the world. They loom large in our imaginations and – just sometimes – also in our memories.

"The climbing was superb. It would have been exceptional on any cliff, but add in the location, the journey to get here and the feeling of reaching the summit of a most extraordinary formation, and we knew this was something else. The ride back in the dinghy that afternoon was a good one."

→ The Free Route (25)
Steve Monks successfully leading the first ascent of pitch one of the first free route on the Totem Pole in 1995.

↑ The Free Route (25)
Simon Mentz leading the first ascent of pitch two of
the free route on the Totem Pole in 1995. Steve Monks
(belaying) and Jane Wilkinson are on the ledge.

→ The Free Route (25)
The day after the first free ascent, Simon Mentz
re-leading pitch two of the route for sunlit photos.
Steve Monks belaying.

← The Ewbank Route (27)
After the establishment of the free route on the Totem Pole, the original 1968 aid route was largely neglected until Doug McConnell and Dean Rollins free climbed it in three pitches in 2009. Here Doug is leading the second pitch with Dean on the hanging belay.

↑ The Sorcerer (27)
Chris Coppard and Garry Phillips established a new three-pitch route on the Totem Pole, which starts by traversing further around the base of the pillar. Here Chris approaches the crux on pitch three, with Garry belaying.

← Ancient Astronaught (24)
The Moai is another formation of note on the Tasman Peninsula in Tasmania, Australia. Compared to the Totem Pole, this 30m pillar offers a couple of easier routes in a more casual setting. Chris Hampton leading with Andy Kuylaars belaying.

← Pole Dancer (22)
This route completes the trilogy of classic pillars found on the Tasman Peninsula (alongside the Totem Pole and the Moai). Located on the Pillars of Hercules at the far end of Cape Raoul, the approach is adventurous and involves hours of hiking, several pitches of climbing, abseils and scrambling, just to reach the start of this superb-quality pitch. Steve Moon climbing.

→ Freedom (30)
Jake Bresnehan on a hard route he established on the dolerite columns of Mount Wellington, Tasmania, Australia.

← Memory Lapse (20)
The Sundial is a neat formation tucked away high up on the hillside of the Remarkables Range, near Queenstown, New Zealand. Ronny Birchler climbing.

→ Saigon Wall (7a)
Lee Cujes climbing on one of the thousands of karsts (limestone towers or islands) in Halong Bay, Vietnam. Though most of the karsts offer little of interest to rock climbers, this one had some quality climbing.

FORMATIONS

↑ **Stolen Chimney (5.11a)**
Monique Forestier proudly atop the Corkscrew
Summit, which is the fifth pitch of this route on the
Ancient Art formation in the Fisher Towers, near
Moab, Utah, USA.

→ **The Cobra (5.11R)**
Chris Donharl preparing the abseil from the summit of
this once-splendid formation. Unfortunately it doesn't
exist anymore, as the formation collapsed at the 'neck'
in a wild storm in 2014. It's also in the Fisher Towers,
near Moab, Utah, USA.

← Baby (7a+)
The mostly conglomerate rock has resulted in perhaps hundreds of curious formations in the Montserrat massif, Spain. Xavier Garcia leading, with Monique Forestier belaying, pitch two of this four-pitch route on the Bessona Inferior formation in the Agulles area.

↓ **Number Two (5.12b)**
John Durr balancing up the Lost Pencil block, far from the road, at Joshua Tree, California, USA.

→ **Norte (6b)**
There are eight pitches of climbing to reach the summit of El Puro pillar at Riglos, Spain. Simon Tappin leading and Nina Leonfellner belaying, with a couple of pitches to go.

INTENSITY

Text by Steve McClure

We climb for a multitude of reasons: the spectacular views, the fresh air, the friendships, the challenge. For those grabbed by the sport, it's often a lifelong relationship, changing and developing over time. Perhaps this is the beauty of the sport; the range and depth of what draws us in. But for me, for now, much of the allure of climbing lies in its intensity.

2

INTENSITY

There are those who push the limits – their own limits. It doesn't have to be the cutting edge. There can be few sports where the best in the world play alongside everyone else, experiencing the same game: the same emotions and the same rewards. My own passion for climbing began with a simple love of the outdoors and the beauty of the movement – even the feel of the texture of the rock – but gradually progressed into the realms of performance. Perhaps unimportant at first, the desire and need to reach the limits, and the buzz of being on top of my game, become an addiction with no cure. The intense medley of physical performance, technical ability and mental strength, all requiring immense depth in their own right. When everything comes together on a journey over stone, there is absolutely nothing better: an experience of incredible intensity.

The desire to perform is a natural progression; with the honeymoon period of the discovery of climbing over, there is often an inbuilt desire to explore one's physical and mental bounds. Most people don't need the extra effort, staying happily married to climbing without ever asking too much, just enjoying its company. But for some, it's what climbing becomes. 'I climb because I can be the best.' Not *the* best, of course, but your best. Climbing is a place where we excel, but it's not elitist – it doesn't care about your numbers relative to others, your top performance being any level that pushes you to the max. Maybe I climb because it brings out my best, it makes me train harder, stay clear headed, stay healthy.

I slipped into 'performance mode' without even noticing. One minute I was happy bumbling around ticking off classics with a pint in the pub and a takeaway pizza, the next it was all about pulling down on tiny crimps, exploding forearms and hanging on till the bitter end, falling lots, but scaling desperately hard routes I'd never have dreamed possible.

My first years of sport climbing were shaped by an intense love affair with the Peak Limestone (the natural crags of the Peak District in the UK) that seemed to fit me perfectly; close to home, fitting around employment, crimpy, powerful, technical and littered with routes I'd spent my entire childhood staring at on the glossy pages of monthly magazines. Big routes with big numbers fell on an unlikely trajectory no one could have imagined: *Zeke* (8b), *Mecca* (8b+), *Make-it-funky* (8c), *Evolution* (8c+). My basecamp became the mighty cliff of Raven Tor, home to some of the world's hardest routes and an intense concentration of test-pieces. Though perhaps not the biggest crag around, each route comes with high demands; if you can climb well at Raven Tor, you can probably climb well anywhere. And as I made the big span sideways to the belay of Jerry Moffat's amazing route *Evolution*, I was already glancing at the obvious blank

"Most people don't need the extra effort, staying happily married to climbing without ever asking too much, just enjoying its company. But for some, it's what climbing becomes. 'I climb because I can be the best.' Not *the* best, of course, but your best."

⟵⟵ The Very Big and the Very Small (8c)
Steve McClure working with holds that don't get much smaller on the Rainbow Slab, Llanberis Slate Quarries, Wales, UK.

⟵ Super Duper Goo (29)
Steve McClure on a route that he onsighted at Diamond Falls in the Blue Mountains, NSW, Australia.

INTENSITY

"In the end it all boiled down to conditions, those tiny crimps only working on the driest and coolest of days – but not too cold, and not too dry! But the real key was to keep a fluent style. Strength and power were simply not enough."

section of rock where the route really should have gone.

Closer inspection revealed perhaps enough features to be climbable. Actually, I knew straight away it was possible – desperate for sure, and close to the edge of not-possible – but that glimmer of potential was one of the most exciting moments in my life. Over the years I've learned to home-in on even the dimmest glows of possibility, to see I might be capable when many climbers would need a far greater chance of success to even begin. In fact, the stacked cards against me were the cause of the thrill. This extension to *Evolution* was going to be punishing; it was likely to take days, weeks, months, even years. I could see that straight away. If it had been easier, I'd still have done it, of course, but it would not have been so special. It would not have been truly hard.

This was to become my first real project. And I define 'real' by one that drifts into multiple years, giving time to reflect and improve and raise your game. Not a short-term project, climbed in a few sessions or even in a season, where you were already good enough right from the start, just needing a little familiarity or some slickness and speed. A real project seeps into your being, becomes the reason you train, the reason you don't eat that extra cake. It's there when you close your eyes at night or have a few moments waiting for the train. How I pored over the moves, analysing in molecular detail how each edge should be taken, and whether perhaps they should be taken in a different way, and how that would affect the next move, and the next ... The final moves were on matchstick edges, so small as to be barely holdable and barely qualifying as a foothold; they only worked with the body in the right place, hips in, trailing foot pressing, chin against the wall.

In the end it all boiled down to conditions, those tiny crimps only working on the driest and coolest of days – but not too cold, and not too dry! But the real key was to keep a fluent style. Strength and power were simply not enough. The second ascensionist and others that tried after all agree, and even with their immense physical strength relative to mine, this route cannot be achieved by just pulling hard on the holds. While I prepared, I kept my hand in at Raven Tor, even on the hot days, the damp days, the misty days and the freezing days, often not even on *my* route, but practising the skills that were required for it. So many days felt a waste of time and energy. But they were all valuable. And when the window of opportunity cracked open, I was ready.

My infatuation with this single line came to a beautiful end; afterwards, I named the route *Mutation*. I can still remember it now – the fingers of my right hand biting hard into the 2-millimetre (0.08-inch) wafer edge, my left foot accurately placed and my right

↗ Mutation (9a)
→ Mecca (8b+)
Steve McClure on two of the test-pieces – including *Mutation*, which he established – at Raven Tor in the Peak District, UK.

INTENSITY

"It shows the power of commitment: to go for a move knowing there is only a one per cent chance of success is awesome, but to really go for it thinking you have no chance at all and to still pull it off is something pretty special; you need something magical to happen."

foot flagged out in that perfect spot calculated over so many sessions. Hips in, and deadpoint upwards with a precise level of force; just enough to make the distance but not so much as to rip your tips straight off the matchsticks. The target: a shallow three-fingertip pocket. On my actual redpoint this final desperate move was so close to the limit that I'm certain a gust of wind blew me upwards just enough to hit the hold. Going into the move I had total conviction, but was sure I was going to be just marginally short. Instead – amazingly – I caught it! It shows the power of commitment: to go for a move knowing there is only a one per cent chance of success is awesome, but to really go for it thinking you have no chance at all and to still pull it off is something pretty special; you need something magical to happen. Relying on a gust of wind would require a monumental leap of faith, not to mention some incredibly fortunate timing.

There are few moments in my life I can remember in such detail. Maybe if I added them all up, I might barely get to sixty seconds. But it's these intense moments that I look back on, and it's these moments that make me really feel alive.

↖ Ring of Fire (8b+)
Steve McClure making the first ascent of what was likely the hardest 'deep-water solo' at the time. Fall badly from this 12m-high route and its name might make more sense. It's located on the Holy Grail Wall, Mana Island, near Kornati, Croatia.

← Ride the Wild Surf (E4, 6a)
Steve McClure on a classic of the Llanberis Slate Quarries, Wales, UK.

↑ **Devil Sticks (5.12b)**
Olivia Hsu flexing on White Mountain, near Yangshuo, China.

↗ **Le Voile de Maya (8c+)**
Didier Berthod committed to hard moves on this route at Rawyl, near Sion, Switzerland.

→ **Reini's Vibos (8c)**
Cristian Brenna has the power to match this thuggish number at Massone, Arco, Italy.

← Punks in the Gym (32)
Mayan Smith-Gobat finding an unusual sequence to unlock the crux of this test-piece at Mount Arapiles, Victoria, Australia. First climbed by Wolfgang Güllich in 1985, this route is widely regarded as the first consensus 32 (5.14a or 8b+) in the world.

→ To Bolt or Not to Be (14a)
Jasna Hodžić navigating this endless sea of crimpers at Smith Rock, Oregon, USA. The route was first climbed in 1986 by Jean-Baptiste Tribout and is considered to be the world's third consensus 32 (5.14a or 8b+).

→ A Gaze Blank and Pitiless as the Sun (30)
Lee Cujes found himself a steep project in the
Summit Caves, high up on Mount Tibrogargan,
in the Glasshouse Mountains, Queensland, Australia.
John J O'Brien belaying.

INTENSITY

↑ Le Blond Project
Chris Sharma attempting a project just to the right of
La Dura Dura, with a likely grade of around 9b+ or 9c,
at Oliana, Spain.

→ La Dura Dura (9b+)
Chris Sharma working his *La Dura Dura* project nearly
a year before his successful ascent of the route;
one of only two graded 9b+ (5.15c or 38) at the time.
The 50m route is at Oliana in Catalunya, Spain.

← Sneaky Snake (33)
Lee Cossey not quite latching the crux on his 55m project, which he climbed on his next attempt, on Taipan Wall, Grampians, Victoria, Australia.

← Hard Candy (27)
Andrew Bull snagging pockets on the steep sandstone of Nowra, NSW, Australia.

↘ Pleasant Screams (26)
Sam Edwards has a tenuous grip on a route that he established on Mount Wellington, Tasmania, Australia.

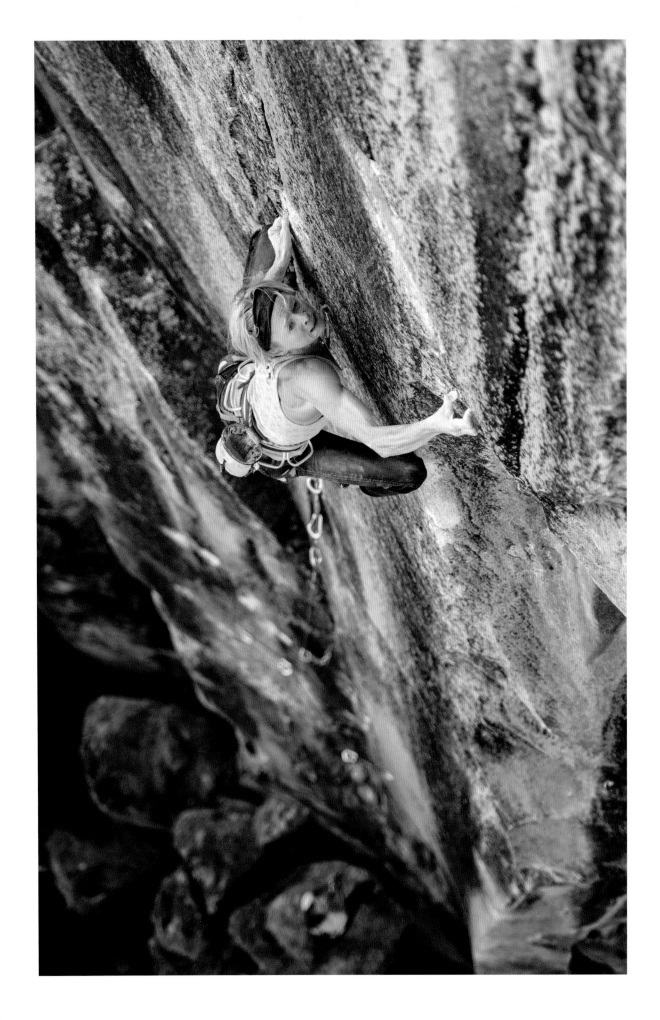

← Whistling Kite (32)
Monique Forestier crimping a minuscule hold on this technical test-piece at Frog Buttress, Queensland, Australia.

→ Il Lungo dei Comanches (7c)
The Valle dell Orco is a granite trad climbing area in northern Italy. Some of the routes are quite long, such as this one on The Corporal. Didier Berthod getting worked on pitch two of this six-pitch route.

← Living on Air (E8 6c)
Mikey Robertson fully committed, high above his last and only protection, during the first ascent of this exceptionally bold route at Stennis Ford, Pembroke, Wales, UK.

→ Wraith (E5 6a)
Tim Emmett intensely focused on one of the classic trad climbs on the unusual fins of Sharpnose in Cornwall, UK.

↓ Saturday Night Palsy (29)
Tracey Hua maxed-out on one of the hardest routes at Mount Ninderry, Queensland, Australia.

ENVIRONMENT

Text by Greg Child

Climbing provides a unique way to experience the wonders of the environment. While it's easy to become absorbed with the immediate challenge of a climb, it's impossible not to be impacted by the majesty of your surroundings. Our connection with nature can become one of the biggest joys of climbing.

3

ENVIRONMENT

At daybreak one November, around 2006, I was camped on the cliffside of Roraima, a mesa in the South American nation of Guyana. This battleship-shaped *tepui*, with its 300-metre (1,000-foot) walls, sat amid rainforest and rivers that fed the Amazon. As shafts of light shot through towering rain clouds, brightening the hard red sandstone around me, I thought about how primally familiar the rock had felt to me these past days of the climb. Not just with my eyes, but also through my fingertips, I was reading Australia's Grampians Range, and the cliffs around Cape Town in South Africa – both places that held special meaning to my climbing psyche. Suddenly it occurred to me that the sense of déjà vu I had been experiencing was proof that the rock I was attached to had, eons ago, been joined to Australia and Africa as a single landmass. The notion of Pangaea had always smacked of Tolkienesque fantasy, and theories of continental drift and plate tectonics, which described vast landmasses floating apart, seemed equally like fables of Middle Earth to my unschooled mind. But there it was, another *Aha!* moment gifted to me through climbing, a reminder that I was no more than a grain of sand in the big picture.

Moving from sand to sea, nostalgia transports me back to 1980, to days spent zooming around the coastal suburbs of Sydney with Australian rockclimber Mike 'Mikl' Law on his Ducati motorbike. Our ropes and gear are strapped to his bike; we're looking for new climbs on the salty sandstone of this urban wilderness. Snippets of the times return: I'm starting up a route right on the cusp of land and sea when a belch of roiling ocean dumps a tonne-weight of water on us. I'm left clinging to wet rock, while Mikl picks himself up off the wave platform. The rope between us is tight – it's held him from being siphoned into the sea. More memories: golf balls flying over our heads as we climb a route beneath a driving range; the snarling of feral cats sunning themselves around an old car chassis that has rusted into the rocks like a melting Dalí clock; midway up a climb a concrete bunker that housed a cannon, from a war long ago. One day, beneath a lighthouse, we find a cliff veiled in a slurry of old concrete, dumped into the sea decades earlier. We try to climb it. We get halfway up. It's a terrible, vulgar climb but the sun and the sea and the ridiculousness of it all make it the best day ever.

The environment looms large in so many of my climbing memories, bringing routes alive so close I can almost touch them. *Excommunication* is a climb that I made the first ascent of, and it sneaks a path up a tower in the Utah desert known as The Priest, which stands at the end of a saw-blade ridge of mesas and spires, above the town I live in, Castle Valley. This is 'red-rock country', where wind and water sculpt canyons and spires into fantastical shapes.

"One day, beneath a lighthouse, we find a cliff veiled in a slurry of old concrete, dumped into the sea decades earlier. We try to climb it. We get halfway up. It's a terrible, vulgar climb but the sun and the sea and the ridiculousness of it all make it the best day ever."

« Twentieth Century Fox (20)
Having climbed the crack, Catherine de Vaus can savour the slab and setting on this classic 50m pitch at Mount Fox in the Grampians, Victoria, Australia.

‹ Excommunication (5.13a)
Greg Child leading, with Renee Globis belaying, the second pitch of the route he established on the aptly named Priest formation, above Castle Valley, near Moab, Utah, USA. Pitches are 5.12b, 5.12a, 5.13a, 5.11b, 5.10d.

It's a curious, anthropomorphic formation, this Priest. Whenever I walk towards it, it seems to lean over me like a wizened instructor meting out rebuke. The Priest was first climbed in 1961 by Layton Kor, Harvey Carter and Annie Carter, via a gaping crack they would call Honeymoon Chimney. When I visited The Priest in 2002 and stood underneath his north face, I saw sunlight glinting off a bone-white shield of calcified stone, revealing a rippling surface that hinted of finger holds. Had I found a route that had eluded others? It was a longshot, but I carried up my equipment and began a long process of climbing up, placing bolts and feeling out the new path. I lived and dreamed that climb for a month, or more.

"When I visited The Priest in 2002 and stood underneath his north face, I saw sunlight glinting off a bone-white shield of calcified stone, revealing a rippling surface that hinted of finger holds. Had I found a route that had eluded others? It was a longshot, but I carried up my equipment and began a long process of climbing up, placing bolts and feeling out the new path. I lived and dreamed that climb for a month, or more."

In the desert most rock is soft. Climbers around this region call such crumbly sandstone 'choss'. Specialists in choss might earn the appellation 'desert rat'. The climbing on *Excommunication* was anything but choss, however; it was solid rock that gave up intricate face climbing for five pitches – one of them at 5.13. But I have a lazy memory for charting climbs with move-by-move language. My brain is wired to recount my times at The Priest with other imagery. I've seen lightning strike its summit, and I've seen climbers on top juggling Saint Elmo's Fire while electricity crackled around them; I hear the sound of a rattlesnake that probably still lives at the base, curled into a tight coil, shaking its tail for all to hear; there are ravens diving like black meteors on currents of air that seethe around the cliffs; and, when darkness descends on a hot summer evening and biting gnats emerge to feast on our skin, I feel the velveteen brush of bat wings across my cheeks and arms as they swoop in to eat the bugs.

Recalling these memories reminds me that we are lucky passengers on a journey that stops briefly to let us visit places that are still wild.

↗ **Excommunication**
Greg Child leading the first pitch (5.12b) of his route on The Priest, Castle Valley, near Moab, Utah, USA.

→ Greg Child interacting with the local environment, near his home in Castle Valley, Utah, USA.

↠ **The Prozac Years (25)**
Greg Child pulling the crux, on the second of three pitches, of a route he established at Shipley Lower in the Blue Mountains, NSW, Australia.

↑ **Anxiety Neurosis (26)**
Mount Arapiles is an oasis among the otherwise flat
farmland of the 'Wimmera' district of western Victoria,
Australia. Here Gareth Llewellin leads pitch two (24) of
this Arapiles classic, with Monique Forestier belaying.

→ **Flaming Hornets (5.12c)**
Yangshuo in China is an incredibly rugged region with
seemingly endless limestone karsts. David Gliddon
making the first ascent of his route at Riverside crag,
next to the Li River.

→ Checkpoint Charlie (21)
Cloud inversion layers are a common occurrence in the Blue Mountains, but don't usually last long in the morning. John Smoothy up early for this route near Katoomba, NSW, Australia.

ENVIRONMENT

↑ **Phyllis Diller (M 10)**
Amazing icicle formations set the scene for
Will Gadd to attempt a hard mixed (rock and
ice) route on the Stanley Headwall, British
Columbia, Canada.

→ **Louise Falls (WI 4)**
A great rock-climbing area in summer, Lake Louise
also provides options when the waterfall freezes in
winter. Abby Watkins starting up the third and final
pitch of one of the most popular ice climbs in the
Rocky Mountains, Alberta, Canada.

→→ **Louise Falls (WI 4)**
Eric Dumerac dislodging ice on pitch three
of the Rocky Mountains classic.

ENVIRONMENT

← **Nine Deep, One Shallow (5.13d)**
Rain washed the smog away to reveal a landscape
where farmers work the patches of fertile flatland
– while climbers play on peaks of steep limestone –
near Yangshuo, China. Monique Forestier climbing
on Banyan Tree Crag.

« Dessert (25)
Jack Masel picking a gap in the rain cells for a late day lap at Wilyabrup in the Margaret River region of Western Australia.

↓ Secret of Beehive (V5)
Hidetaka Suzuki climbing his high-ball boulder problem in the Buttermilk Boulders, near Bishop, California, USA.

→ Propellerhead (7c)
Jvan Tresch not letting a little slush deter a bouldering session at Sustenpass, Uri, Switzerland.

ENVIRONMENT

← Manara-Potsiny (8a)
Toni Lamprecht up early on the eighth pitch of the
600m route he helped establish on Tsaranoro Be,
one of the enormous granite domes of the Tsaranoro
massif, Madagascar.

← Loose Lady (5.9)
Doug Acorn slabbing up the Houser Buttress at
Joshua Tree, California, USA.

↑ Figures on a Landscape (5.10b)
Greg Loniewski following with Kate Rutherford
belaying on pitch one of the North Astro Dome
classic at Joshua Tree, California, USA.

ENVIRONMENT

← **Make it Snappy**
Monique Forestier attempting pitch three of a seemingly abandoned five-pitch project on Berhala Island, off the coast of Borneo, Malaysia. The first three pitches are 6c, 7b+, 7c and the grade of the last two is unknown.

↓ Tafo Masina (8a)
Fred Moix attempts a short but tricky roof on Nosy Anjombalova island, one of the twelve that comprise the Nosy Hara Archipelago off the coast of northern Madagascar. Surrounded by coral reefs, the islands are part of an important marine-protected area.

→ Jesus Built My Hotrod (27)
Bruce Dowrick climbing at Little Babylon crag in the picturesque Cleddau Valley near Milford Sound on New Zealand's South Island.

↘ Contact Neurosis (29)
Matt Evrard climbing at Chasm Crag, Cleddau Valley near Milford Sound on South Island, New Zealand.

↑ **Zasle Casy**
The Teplicke-Adršpach Rock Park in the Czech Republic (or Czechia) is a historic climbing area comprising hundreds of spires and towers. A unique set of climbing ethics – and bold style – has evolved to protect the soft sandstone from damage; for example, metal protection is not allowed in cracks. Miras Mach leading a route of Czech grade VIIIa (about French 6b+).

→ **Per Elisa (6b+)**
Klemen Kejžar leading a sport route at Cinque Torri in the Dolomites, Italy.

LINES

Text by Alison Osius

Strong lines make for compelling climbs. The route could be a crack, a corner, a dyke or simply a coloured stripe of rock. Drawn to a particular line, climbers are forced to deal with whatever is required. Routes with strong, beautiful lines can become missions or even obsessions.

4

The best line I ever saw was Cenotaph Corner on Dinas Cromlech, a sculpted, perfect open book, 37 metres (120 feet) tall and set high up the steep scree slopes of Llanberis Pass in North Wales. *The Corner* is the most obvious route in the Pass, clearly visible from the road. The best-known route in the United Kingdom, it was likely the greatest climb ever done by Joe Brown, so renowned he once received a letter addressed simply to 'The Human Fly, Llanberis, North Wales.' The route is famous for its symmetry, commanding position and history. In the same way that people remember major national events, climbers remember when they did *The Corner*.

My time on the route spanned an important chapter for me, a period that solidified the role of climbing in my life, when a short summer visit to Wales as a college student led to another the next year upon graduation. What was intended as 'probably two months' of climbing became four or five, followed by 'just one more' season guiding and then three summers after that. Avocation naturally became vocation, and I worked as an editor at several climbing magazines from 1988 until 2022.

I have climbed on Cenotaph Corner twice. Pursuing this striking line has been part of my appreciation of the sport – from following in the footsteps of Joe Brown, who made the first ascent, to finding a kindred spirit in the film director Tony Scott, when upon mention of the route, a pleasant conversation suddenly transitioned into something much deeper.

Joe Brown was aged eighteen and had only been climbing a few years during his first attempt on *The Corner* in 1948. He and his friends would protect their climbs by placing stones in cracks (he tucked small stones into his balaclava for the purpose) and slinging them, attaching loops of cord for safety; in time Joe began picking up nuts on railroad tracks to use. Starting up *The Corner* the first time, unfazed that the country's top climbers had not ventured upon the route, nor that it was winter, Joe took five pitons and a mason's hammer. He passed the first hard section at 6 metres (20 feet) and managed a tricky move into a niche at about 30 metres (100 feet). Exiting the niche is the route's crux. Trying to place a peg, he dropped the hammer, which hit his belayer Wilf White on the head. Joe hurried down his rope, hand over hand, to find his friend discombobulated but conscious. Wilf urged him back up; Joe tried, but had used up all his pitons (and luck).

Joe returned with his fellow climber Doug Belshaw in August 1952. As Joe would later write in his memoir, *The Hard Years*: 'Getting into the niche at 100 feet was absolutely gripping – very much harder than I remembered it ... The exit crack jutted out above.' He tried an assortment of pins, buckling them, and thought, as he recalled,

"My time on the route spanned an important chapter for me, a period that solidified the role of climbing in my life, when a short summer visit to Wales as a college student led to another the next year upon graduation."

> "The account reads: 'There was a large jug-handle hold above. If I used it, releasing a hand from the crack would swing me off. But I had to use it or fall off.' He grabbed the jug, wrenched on it, and launched upward."

'Oh, damn it, you'll have to bridge up across the bulge to ... bang one in higher up.'

He wedged a peg 'loosely' in the crack at his level and pulled sideways off it, a move 'as hard as any I had done in my life. The last thing I expected was to be able to stay suspended in so fantastic a position' – but he did, and hammered in a big peg above the impending rock. He pasted his stockinged feet against the left wall. Yes, he climbed the damp rock – for its first ascent – in socks.

The account reads: 'There was a large jug-handle hold above. If I used it, releasing a hand from the crack would swing me off. But I had to use it or fall off.' He grabbed the jug, wrenched on it, and launched upward.

I tried the route in 1979, knowing it would be a very hard lead for me. It also happened to be the day Ron Fawcett, then *the* UK climber, dressed in electric-green tank top and shorts, climbed the adjacent, forbidding *Lord of the Flies* for the BBC. 'Come on, arms, do your stuff,' he muttered at the crux, a line that sparked fond hilarity among climbers across the land (he would not even remember saying it).

The camera crew, not at the moment filming, idly watched my effort. I passed the first crux, eventually gained the niche, and tried to move up and around the bulge, clipping the old Joe Brown pin. Did I know or think to back it up with a piece of protection of my own? I doubt it. I had not taken many (any?) leader falls at that point; I remember thinking, *I guess this is all part of it.* Trying to climb above the pin – at perhaps 5 metres (16 feet) below the anchor – I fell, whistling down some 6 metres (15 or 20 feet).

'Use the peg!' my friend Matthew called, asking that I pull or stand on the piton for aid.

That would have been cheating – as if I wasn't by falling, but I did want to manage the moves – and I tried again, flailed and fell again – maybe twice more. 'Use the peg!' Matthew called more urgently. I hesitated. 'Use the fucking peg!' called the entire BBC camera crew.

A year later, I travelled to North Wales to climb and guide. Arriving in early July and staying until November, I enjoyed one of the greatest learning and experiential times of my life.

Climbing continually, I improved more than I had dared expect, and at some point that summer, silent with apprehension and anticipation, embarked on *The Corner* again. Proceeding, I was thrilled to exit the niche, yet shocked to find the very last moves as hard as they were. The route is UK 5c and by then I was climbing that grade and used to the area rock, but I still remember gaping at those slick divots as my arms began to flame. In haste I gave it everything, and scraped by; realizing a dream.

← Belly Full of Bad Berries (5.13a)
John Varco fighting this nauseating offwidth crack at Indian Creek, Utah, USA.

Over the years I worked at *Climbing* magazine, and, while there, I also became the president of the American Alpine Club (AAC). One of the issues facing us at the time occurred in 1998 when the Forest Service announced it would disallow the use of bolts by climbers on the wilderness lands it administered. Among the many places to be affected were the grand multi-pitch cliffs of Suicide and Tahquitz, Southern California.

One afternoon a woman in Los Angeles called my office and asked if I could take a call from Tony Scott. Though a film buff, I didn't then know the name. She said he was a director, with films that included *Top Gun* and *Crimson Tide*. 'He's pretty famous,' she said kindly.

Tony came on the line: British accent, friendly and peppy. He said that he was a climber, and he'd grown up in England and learned at venues throughout the UK. He now frequented Suicide and Tahquitz, and he asked what he could do to help with the Forest Service issue.

We chatted, getting acquainted. I said I'd climbed in Scotland, England and North Wales, and we each waxed effusive about Llanberis Pass. I don't know which of us brought up Cenotaph Corner, but at some point he said, 'I soloed it, actually.' I was stunned. 'You soloed *The Corner*? The hardest moves are at the top!' He laughed and said, 'Well, yes, they are.' I asked more, and we talked on. At one point he paused and said, 'You know, it's really nice to talk to another climber.'

Over time, with pride and interest, I watched Tony Scott's *Spy Game*, *The Taking of Pelham 123* and *Man on Fire*. Oddly, I had never seen *Top Gun* until November 2022, when I watched the sequel, *Top Gun: Maverick*. I was much moved by the homage to the brilliant opening of the original.

In the months since, I have thought often about Tony. In 2012 I read that he had jumped to his death off a bridge in Los Angeles Harbor. He was sixty-eight, had a wife and twin boys. The impetus was not disclosed.

He had rock climbed for decades, and still climbed. That day, he charged up a 5-metre (15-foot) wall on the bridge framework, solid in his climbing movement. A woman watching thought it was a movie stunt. Heartsick, I wrote a short obituary of him for *Rock and Ice* magazine's annual tribute to Climbers We Lost.

Cenotaph Corner is a great line that connected me, if briefly, to a great. Tony and I had shared an appreciation and an understanding of something early and exceptional that he had done. I think of the focus he must have had, then and ever.

> "One afternoon a woman in Los Angeles called my office and asked if I could take a call from Tony Scott. Though a film buff, I didn't then know the name. She said he was a director, with films that included *Top Gun* and *Crimson Tide*. 'He's pretty famous,' she said kindly."

→ **Grand Wall (5.11a)**
Abby Watkins leading the infamous Split Pillar (5.10b), the sixth pitch of this ten-pitch route, on the Stawamus Chief, Squamish, BC, Canada. Sean Isaac belaying.

← Redline (28)
Malcolm Matheson revved-up on a beautiful
line he found at The Lost World, The Grampians,
Victoria, Australia.

↑ Infirmity (23)
Malcolm Matheson dancing up one of the few crack
lines that go the full height of the aptly named Great
Wall at Moonarie, South Australia.

→ Apline (13)
Roxanne Wells climbs without rope on *the*
line of White Water Wall, Freycinet Peninsula,
Tasmania, Australia.

↓ Black Dyke (5.13b)
Matt Maddaloni, having previously made the first
free ascent of the lower (crux) pitches, leading the
sixth pitch (5.12a) of this obvious line. Eleven pitches
in total, it ascends the Stawamus Chief, Squamish,
BC, Canada.

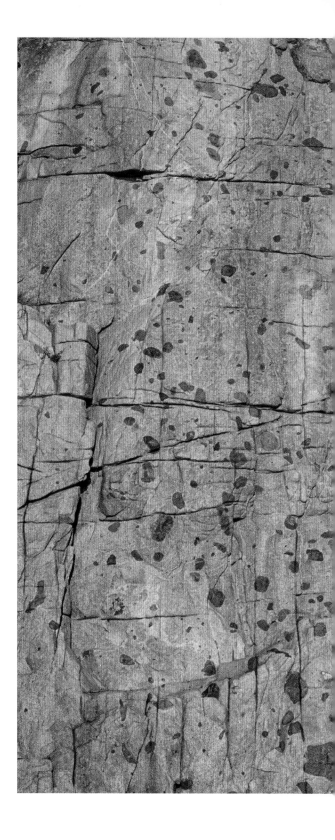

'My name is Ozymandias, king of kings:
Look on my works, ye Mighty, and despair!'
The king line of Mount Buffalo's 270m-high North
Wall is undoubtedly the original *Ozymandias* route
combined with the *Ozymandias Direct* to finish. Steve
Monks made the first free ascent of both variations,
which combine to give pitch grades of 23, 28, 25, 24,
22, 28, 23, 10 and 24. Here Steve is on pitch two, with
Enga Lokey belaying.

→ Ozymandias Direct (28)
Steve Monks leading pitch six of the combined direct
at Mount Buffalo, Victoria, Australia.

Trilogy of trad cracks in the Blue Mountains,
NSW, Australia.

↑ Catch the Wind (21)
Brittany Griffith catching a break on this strange
two-pitch corner crack at Engineer's Cascade.

→ Grasshopper (25)
Mike Law on pitch two of this fine three-pitch line that
he free climbed at Pierce's Pass.

↠ Janicepts (21)
Nicky Dyal punching up the Mount Piddington classic.
Free climbed by Mike Law in 1973, it was the first route
of its grade in the country.

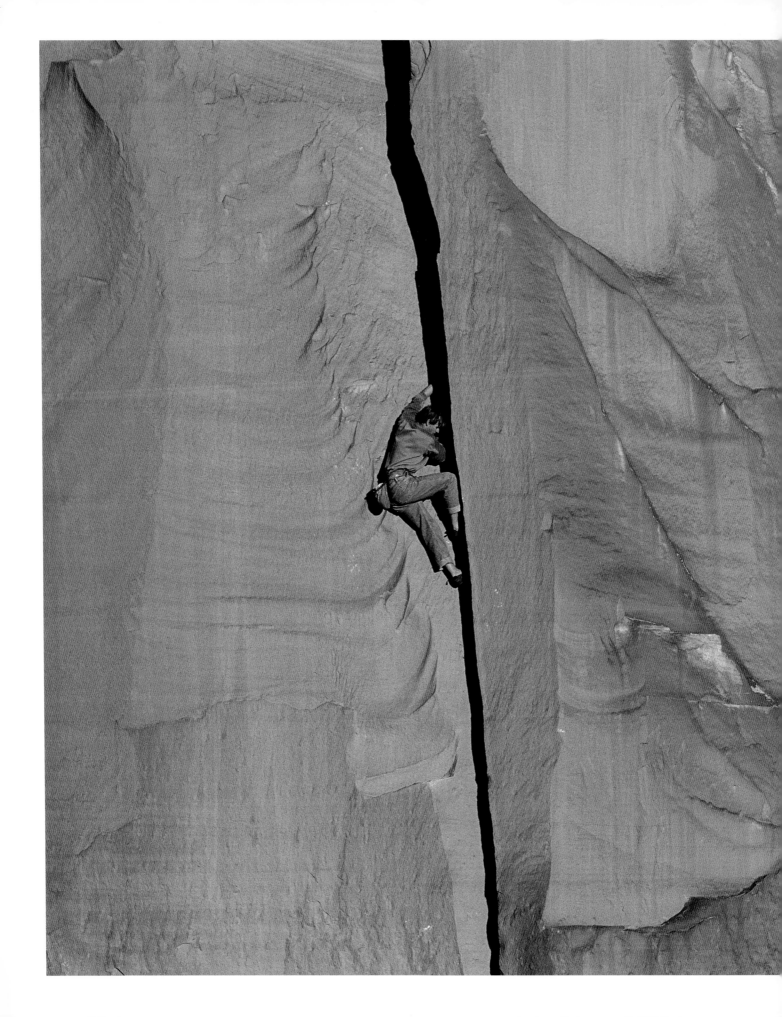

←← Tweety (5.10)
Jason Smith soloing up (then down) this line at
Cat Wall, Indian Creek, Utah, USA.

↑ Humildes pa Casa (8b+)
Tufas can make great lines too. Guillaume Lebret on
this sustained test-piece at Oliana, Spain.

→ Tom et je Ris (8b+)
Monique Forestier utilizing the tufa line that has made
this 60m abseil-in climb-out route in the Verdon
Gorge, France, both possible and so appealing. Alan
Carne belaying.

The incredible hexagonal columns of Devil's Tower, Wyoming, USA, have resulted in many perfectly formed, long and sustained climbs. These are two of the classics.

← **Mr Clean (5.11a)**
Brittany Griffith climbing.

→ **El Matador (5.10d)**
Crystal Davis climbing.

ARÊTES

Text by Amity Warme

Arête is a French word meaning 'spine of the mountain' or sharp ridge. In rock climbing, it's commonly used to describe the outer edge of a corner – an outside corner if you like. Perhaps a knife blade of rock sticking out into space, open air all around, arêtes provide some of the most intimidating and outrageous situations that climbers can find themselves in. They make for inspiring lines and, more often than not, exciting climbs.

5

Latch the hold, take a breath, relax my body, clip the quickdraw, squeeze the arête, build my feet, balance, repeat. My body feels the rhythm of this intricate dance as I visualize the moves of *Sarchasm*, a stunning 5.14a arête climb in Rocky Mountain National Park, Colorado.

Situated at the base of one of the most impressive alpine rock walls in North America and adjacent to a large, blue glacier lake, *Sarchasm* is a striking line that captures the attention and begs to be climbed. I had been incredibly inspired by this route for a long time, but also felt immensely daunted by the challenge it presented. Not only would it be my first of the grade, but it also sits at an elevation of over 3,600 metres (12,000 feet) and is guarded by a steep 13.5-kilometre (8.5-mile) round-trip hike. I was intimidated to try, but I knew that projecting *Sarchasm* would require me to grow as a climber, and I was eager for that progression. I first tried the route in the summer of 2021, but only briefly explored the moves before concluding that it was completely out of my league. Even individual moves felt out of reach. The next summer, I returned with a greater level of intention – I truly wanted to focus on this line and apply myself to the challenge. I was eager to test myself, learn from the process and to find out if I was capable of sending this difficult arête, first climbed by Tommy Caldwell many years back.

The route starts with a brutally crimpy boulder problem, then transitions to technical climbing as you balance back and forth on the sharp arête. There are minimal holds and the crux requires sequential pinching, pushing and pulling as you navigate the fine balance between staying on and falling off. Your body position rarely feels secure as you fight to believe your feet won't skate off the tiny granite crystals. Arête climbing is a unique style that demands a precise combination of both technique and strength. Technical prowess and creativity allow you to use the edge of the arête for toe hooking, heel hooking and balance. Strength allows you to use the corner and any subtle features on the face for laybacking, crimping and locking off between moves. As I engaged in the process of trying *Sarchasm*, it became clear that I needed to add more skills to my climbing repertoire, both physical and mental.

One trait I had to foster was self-belief, which I achieved partly through learning to visualize the climb. Between coordinating partners and the weather and my schedule and the arduous approach, I was only climbing on the route one or two days a week during the month I was working on it, so every go mattered. It was not nearly as many days as I would have liked, so towards the end of the process I really recognized the importance of visualization. It was not just about picturing the moves themselves, but also about how I wanted to feel throughout the climb: calm, confident, strong, balanced, determined.

"Your body position rarely feels secure as you fight to believe your feet won't skate off the tiny granite crystals. Arête climbing is a unique style that demands a precise combination of both technique and strength."

← **Black Gold (25)**
Monique Forestier leading a disconcertingly sharp arête at Corroboree Walls in the Blue Mountains, NSW, Australia.

→ **Chain Reaction (5.12c)**
Amity Warme leading this overhanging arête that is one of most iconic lines at Smith Rock, Oregon, USA.

ARÊTES

Beyond being physically capable, I had to *believe* that I could do this climb. Stamina, finger strength and technical skills were critical, but self-belief was equally important.

That's one of the beautiful aspects of climbing. It provides a space to practise self-belief. By choosing a challenging goal, we give ourselves the opportunity to improve not only in the physical sense, but also in our mental approach. Pursuing a big goal is humbling and rewarding, intimidating and motivating. In the midst of the process there are days when you chart heaps of progress and days when you seem to be moving backwards. Accomplishing a goal that is personally very difficult requires riding out those highs and lows, staying in the process and not giving up: not letting go of the dream. Climbing an arête requires balance – leaning one way, then the other – flowing through a careful sequence of pushing, pulling, squeezing, building and breathing. In a similar way, there is a balance to be found in the mental side of climbing. It is no easy feat learning how to care so much about a goal that you will pour your heart, time, money and effort into it, yet not become so attached that the outcome defines you. It's a tricky balance to care deeply about something, to work hard for a certain result, but not tether your self-worth to success.

Choosing goals like *Sarchasm* – ones that stretch me both physically and mentally – is a perfect experience through which to practise this balance. It is also an integral part of my development as a climber and as a person. Ultimately, I am drawn to big wall climbing where a vast repertoire of climbing skills is crucial to success. Exploring a wide variety of climbing styles – from overhangs to crack lines, arêtes and everything in between – helps prepare me for any challenge that I might encounter when questing up a big wall. In addition to learning the physical skills to tackle any style, it is necessary to cultivate the belief that I can handle a difficult pitch in the middle of a big objective. Practising that self-belief on smaller goals sets me up for success when I pursue bigger goals later on. Every experience builds on the previous one as I seek to become the best climber I can be.

The day I sent *Sarchasm*, I climbed the route exactly how I had visualized it so many times before. My mind and body knew exactly what to do. Exactly when to latch the hold, take a breath, relax my body, clip the draw, squeeze the arête, build my feet, balance, repeat. I had learned what I needed from this striking arête in the mountains of Colorado. I improved as a climber and I was reminded just how powerful a tool the mind is in our climbing performance. It's not enough to want something. It's not even enough to work hard for something. You also have to *believe* that you are capable.

"The day I sent *Sarchasm*, I climbed the route exactly how I had visualized it so many times before. My mind and body knew exactly what to do. Exactly when to latch the hold, take a breath, relax my body, clip the draw, squeeze the arête, build my feet, balance, repeat."

← Our Terminal World (25)
Heather Lawton staying focused on this overhanging, undercut, sandy and exposed arête at Point Perpendicular, NSW, Australia.

↑ Bod Zlomu
Luboš Mázl attempting a sparsely bolted arête
(Czech grade Xc, French 8a+) on Chrámové Stěny,
Teplicke-Adršpach Rock Park, Czechia.

→ Lebensraum (25)
Malcolm Matheson high on a two-pitch that he
established on Mount Buffalo, Victoria, Australia.

← **The Regular Route (25)**
This airy arête, on the penultimate pitch of this 190m route, is situated above the Grose Valley in the Blue Mountains, NSW, Australia. Pitches are graded 23, 25, 24, 21, 24, 22 and 23. Cherry Baylosis leading with Monique Forestier belaying.

→ **Outside Chance (16)**
Rob Saunders enjoying the relative jug-haul up the arête forming the left end of the Great Wall at Moonarie in the Flinders Ranges, South Australia.

ARÊTES

← **Arête de Marseille (5c)**
After an hour hiking in, sunrise finds Nadine Rousselot (leading) and Mathieu Geoffray (belaying) already on pitch two of this five-pitch Calanques classic, first climbed in 1927. It's on La Grande Candelle, overlooking the Mediterranean, France.

↑ Ni Teva Ni Meva (6c+)
Anders Lantz pulling on pebbles of La Momia
formation, Sant Benet area, Montserrat, Spain.

→ Delagokante
A gap in the clouds reveals Dave Russell (leading)
and Rico Miledi (belaying) on this four-pitch route
that was first climbed in 1911 and graded UIAA grade
IV+ or French grade 4. This is the South West Arête
of the Delago Tower, the Vajolet Towers, Rosengarten
– in the Italian Dolomites.

↑ The Golden Pillar of Fortescue (25)
Steve Monks leading the third of four pitches during
the first ascent of this route near Fortescue Bay on
the Tasman Peninsula, Tasmania, Australia.

→ L'île aux Trésors (6b+)
While Jean-François Reffet climbed this nice arête,
the boatman snorkelled and caught lobster for our
dinner. It's on Nosy Anjombalova, part of the Nosy
Hara Archipelago, Madagascar.

⇇ Until the Cows Come Home (26)
Monique Forestier enjoying a recent and atypical
addition to the offerings at Mount Piddington, in the
Blue Mountains, NSW, Australia.

↑ Body Count Extension (24)
Ben Wiessner savouring a neat little arête at the end
of this route at Van Dieman's Land, in the Grampians,
Victoria, Australia.

→ Wheels of Steel (27)
Ashlee Hendy is the early bird on this plum
line at Koalasquatsy Crag in the Grampians,
Victoria, Australia.

ARÊTES

↑ Fun Terminal (5.12a)
Hans Florine enjoying this novelty sport route up the
arête of the Killer Pillar, Yosemite, California, USA.

→ Spank the Monkey (5.13d)
Mike Doyle testing himself on the hard and run-out
arête of the Monkey Face, Smith Rock, Oregon, USA.

← Soul Catcher (25)
Stefan Glowacz onsighting this fine arête at Porter's Pass, Blue Mountains, NSW, Australia. Ben Cossey manning the hanging belay.

↓ Naked and Disfigured (5.12b)
Tae Kim climbing one of the premium lines at Jane's Wall, Red Rocks, near Las Vegas, Nevada, USA.

→ Pokamoko and the Valley Girl (31)
Duncan Steel on this soaring technical arête, one of the area test-pieces at Frog Buttress, Queensland, Australia.

WALLS

Text by Liv Sansoz

The walls I've encountered during my life as a climber have taken many forms, from the intimidating overhangs of competition walls to the smooth expanses of limestone sport crags and the endless granite sweeps of big walls. While for some people a wall might symbolize an obstacle, I see a challenge.

6

WALLS

"As I took my competition climbing game to real rock, once again I would find myself standing at the foot of a wall, feeling dwarfed by the blank face rising above me. The question of whether I had what it took coexisted in my mind with a burning desire to rise to the challenge and find my way up."

Steep, blank walls have always inspired me to formulate strategies to reach the top. I've often felt small and vulnerable standing at the foot of a wall, but my secret weapon is my ability to transform that feeling into a desire to reach the summit. It might look hard, but I know I'll find a way.

The first walls that left a real impression on me were competition walls. It gave me goose bumps to stand at the base of a wall and look up at the route. Was I strong enough? Was I smart enough to figure out the puzzle that had been created just for us? Once my feet left the ground, the questions ended and my inner warrior came alive. I was fuelled by what felt like a superpower, originating somewhere deep inside of me. Nothing could interrupt the trance of my concentration. As I gained experience, my mental game got better and better. The internal chatter was silenced, replaced by a mental image of myself on the wall, as if I were outside of my own body, watching from afar. In my last year of competition climbing, everything went like clockwork. I was strong and I knew how to manage the pressure. Once shielded by my bubble of concentration, the only thing that mattered was getting to the top of the wall. Back then a 'super final' would be held in the case of a tie, so I always hoped there would be two tops in the last round so I would get to climb the super final route. When everything flowed it no longer felt like climbing; it felt like floating.

As I took my competition climbing game to real rock, once again I found myself standing at the foot of a wall, feeling dwarfed by the blank face rising above me. The question of whether I had what it took coexisted in my mind with a burning desire to rise to the challenge and find my way up. Outside, smooth clean limestone walls suited me best. Everyone brings a little bit of their personality to their climbing. Both on the rock and off it, I enjoy precision. If you want to climb demanding routes on the pure limestone walls of the Virgin River Gorge (USA), Cimaï, Buoux, Céüse and the Gorges du Tarn (all in France), you have to be precise, meticulous and focused, even while you're fighting the pump. *Necessary Evil*, in the Virgin River Gorge, was exactly that kind of route. I had every move dialled down to the millimetre, from the exact position of my hips as I flagged, to the tiny thumb catch that made a seemingly impossible move possible. I've always found it incredibly satisfying to get to the point where I've memorized everything perfectly, from the body position to the rhythm, to the amount of pressure on each hold. That feeling of moving with total focus and exactitude up a smooth, clean wall is unforgettable. In that moment, you aren't so much a climber as the conductor of a symphony of movement.

But in spite of all my perfectly dialled micro-beta, not everything was within my control. I was probably just a couple of

← ← Project (9a)
Chris Sharma attempting pitch four of his 250m multi-pitch project at Mont-rebei, Spain. Tentative pitch grades are 6c+, 9a, 8b, 8c, 8c, 7b, 8c+. Klemen Bečan belaying.

← Octopus (7c+)
Liv Sansoz climbing on the pocketed limestone walls of the Gorges du Tarn, Lozère, France. The name of this sector, Güllich (named after the great Wolfgang Güllich), gives a good hint as to the powerful nature of the climbing.

tries away from sending *Necessary Evil* when I was dropped by my belayer while lowering off the warm-up. I fractured a vertebra, which brought my stay in the States to an abrupt end. The injury changed the path of my climbing career, but ultimately led me to discover a different kind of wall: the big wall.

At the foot of a hulking granite big wall, more than anywhere else, you can't help but feel small as you crane your neck to stare up at the face. And once again, when met with this obstacle, I saw a challenge that I could not refuse. There are a lot of unknowns when it comes to big wall climbing, but I always feel confident that together with my climbing partners, we'll be able to find solutions and make the right decisions. My trip to Yosemite in 2013 with my paraplegic friend Vanessa François and fellow team members Marion Poitevin and Fabien Dugit was no exception. The atypical challenge and unusual circumstances made the trip one of the most remarkable experiences of my climbing career. This time the goal wasn't the individual achievement of redpointing a route or winning a competition, but the shared project of helping Vanessa get to the top of the huge granite giant that is El Capitan. We would have to pool our energy, knowledge, skills and experience if we wanted it to be a success.

Vanessa, an accomplished alpine climber before her accident, approached me after her rehabilitation process because she wanted to find a way to keep climbing in spite of her disability. She put together a team of climbers and we spent two years preparing for the trip. The project involved a huge amount of fundraising, planning and logistics, so while it wasn't a matter of focusing on the individual moves the way you would on a techy face climb, there were still a whole lot of details to get right. How would Vanessa get to the foot of the wall? How would she transfer from the rope to the portaledge at the end of every pitch? How would she get down from the summit? What if something went wrong? We had to be meticulous and resourceful as we developed our strategy to make Vanessa's crazy dream of climbing the *Zodiac* on El Capitan come true.

After two years of preparation, we finally arrived in the States, only to find ourselves in the midst of a government budget shutdown that restricted access to Yosemite National Park. As a group of French climbers, we didn't understand the significance of the shutdown, so when we discovered that the park's gates were open, we went for it. The upside was that Yosemite was deserted, and for five days we were the only team on what is usually one of the busiest big walls in the world. It was an emotional moment as we watched Vanessa leave the ground, making the first of countless pull-ups that it would take to climb the 650-metre (2,133-foot) face.

"There are a lot of unknowns when it comes to big wall climbing, but I always feel confident that together with my climbing partners, we'll be able to find solutions and make the right decisions."

↗ **Les Nouvelles Plantations du Christ (7c+)**
Liv Sansoz on this long pumpy 35m pitch; an area classic. If that's not enough, the extension adds 20m and another grade. It's on Tennessee Wall, Gorges du Tarn, Lozère, France.

→ **Nom de Mostuéjouls! (7b)**
Liv Sansoz on one of the long 35m pitches at Tennessee Wall, Gorges du Tarn, Lozère, France.

"After five days of edging our way stubbornly up the wall, we finally found ourselves dazed and grinning at the summit, each of us transformed by the magical energy that comes from achieving something totally improbable, together."

We were soon four tiny specks of humanity lost on a sea of granite, isolated from the world below. Whether you're fighting your way up a competition wall, tick tacking up an immaculate piece of limestone or inching your way up a big wall, that singular feeling of being in your own bubble is a remarkable one. It's a kind of isolation that feels reassuring rather than stressful. On a big wall, life is reduced to just the essential tasks: climbing, hauling, eating, drinking, sleeping and getting up the next day to do it all again. In our case, none of these mundane tasks proved simple. We dealt with an endless series of unexpected complications, from rope tangles of epic proportions to sudden gusts of wind that sent the portaledge flying like a kite as we hauled it from one anchor to the next.

The craziest thing of all was that in spite of all the obstacles, the harmony and symbiosis between Vanessa, Marion, Fabien and me was unlike anything I'd ever experienced. After five days of edging our way stubbornly up the wall, we finally found ourselves dazed and grinning at the summit, each of us transformed by the magical energy that comes from achieving something totally improbable, together.

Perhaps the beauty of climbing a wall, whatever kind of wall it may be, boils down to this: finding the motivation and confidence to take on the challenge, building a bubble of calm and concentration, focusing on the details with care and precision, and digging deep to summon energy you didn't know you had. Put these pieces together and what should be a rough struggle against gravity feels like grace.

→ Zodiac (A2 5.7 or 5.13d)
Alex Huber making a blistering fast 2h31m20s ascent of the 600m route *Zodiac*, with his brother Thomas Huber (out of frame). In 2003, it set a new speed record for an ascent of El Capitan in Yosemite, California, USA. Here, Alex is racing up pitch fourteen of the sixteen-pitch route. Having reached the previous belay ledge, Alex has tied off the rope with about 20m of slack piled up on the ledge – and has kept climbing – while Thomas is climbing the fixed rope to the belay.

↗ Alex barely pausing to place some protection on pitch fifteen.

Sandstone walls of the Grose Valley in the Blue Mountains, NSW, Australia.

↑ **Wild Wild West (23)**
Vince Day leading a 45m route on the aptly named Great Outdoors Wall at Hanging Rock.

→ **Big Nose (26)**
Flint Duxfield extending himself on the 'Spine Chiller traverse' on pitch seven (21) of this 250m route at Pierce's Pass.

⇢ **I Have a Dream (25)**
Vince Day climbing an imaginative abseil-in climb-out route at Pierce's Pass.

WALLS

← Simply the Best (28)
Andrew Cubbon attempting one of the brilliant sport routes at The Star Factory, Freycinet Peninsula, Tasmania, Australia.

↓ Training for Big Walls (19)
Jean-Philippe Dumas nearing halfway of this two-pitch route on the atmospheric Southern Ocean Wall, West Cape Howe, Western Australia.

→ Talk is Cheap (24)
Garry Phillips leading the second (and crux) of ten pitches on the adventurous 210m abseil-in climb-out route that he co-authored on the main face of Mount Brown, Tasman Peninsula, Tasmania, Australia. Jake Bresnehan belaying.

WALLS

← Daedalus (29)
Monique Forestier keeping cool through massive
run-outs on the stunning marbled sandstone of
Taipan Wall in the Grampians, Victoria, Australia.

WALLS

↓　Land Art (7c)
Cristian Brenna leading pitch three (7b) of four, on the
aesthetic Transatlantico crag – one of the many crags
around Arco, Italy. Fabio Leoni belaying.

→　Golden Ticket (5.14c)
Matty Hong on his way to claim this prized test-piece
of the Red River Gorge, Kentucky, USA.

← License to Climb Harder (7c)
Lee Cujes found the limestone on this wall – like dripping candle wax – so enjoyable to climb that he added an extension. Gracing one of the thousands of islands in Halong Bay, Vietnam, the wall is named The Face.

← Bachar-Yerian (5.11c)
Stefan Schiller hanging on for the clip – with his last piece of protection at the bottom of the frame – during his onsight of this notorious, exceptionally bold route. This is the second of four pitches. Established ground-up in the 1980s, it's on Medlicott Dome in Tuolumne Meadows, Yosemite National Park, CA, USA.

→ Shipoopi! (5.11d)
Something of a companion route to the Bachar-Yerian – just to its left, though far more generously protected – is this one on the beautiful knobby granite of Medlicott Dome. Heidi Wirtz is leading pitch two with David Bloom belaying.

← Flight of the Phoenix (18)
AJ Brown leading, with Jacob Greber belaying,
somewhere on this classic 310m adventure route on
Bluff Mountain in the Warrumbungles, NSW, Australia.

↑ Eve Line (7b)
Arnaud Petit on the limestone walls of Verdon Gorge,
Alpes de Provence, France. Stéphanie Bodet belaying.

→ Flaming Galah (30)
Kumari Barry working the sixth (crux) pitch of this
230m route on the South Wall of Bungonia Gorge,
NSW, Australia. James Alexander belaying.

FLOW

Text by Daila Ojeda

In those perfect moments when the difficulty of a climb matches our skill level, we enter a state of flow – fully absorbed, we shed our self-consciousness. When you are 'in the zone', climbing becomes automatic; it creates a focus that takes us into the present moment and away from the noise and distractions of everyday life.

7

The first thing that comes to mind when we think about the skills required for rock climbing is physical strength, and we're not wrong: climbing requires strength, endurance and flexibility ... but there are plenty of other relevant tools that allow us to progress more efficiently as climbers. This was a huge discovery for me.

I started climbing on the island of my birth, Gran Canaria. The volcanic rock of the Canary Islands is very aesthetic, characterized by the dark colour of basalt. I initially fell in love with the sport because I was drawn to the lifestyle – a community that spent its time outdoors in nature. From the beginning, climbing itself represented a real challenge for me. I remember feeling frustrated and out of my comfort zone. I was used to playing sports, having done so since I was a child, so I felt physically capable – but I was scared when I climbed. Even though this fear prevented me from moving forwards, I couldn't stop thinking about the next time I could go climbing again. It wasn't until a few years later and thanks to a good friend that I understood that my block was mental. I was putting my attention solely on the physical part of the game.

One of the great lessons I've learned through climbing is to keep my mind in the present moment. Focus starts with a goal; to succeed, you have to lead your thoughts in the direction of that ambition. When I climb, I try to pay attention to the sequence of moves right in front of me, to focus on the problems that I have to solve without thinking about what comes next, for that belongs to the future. My aim is not usually to complete the ascent; I want to, of course, but the end result is the consequence of achieving a series of smaller goals that help me to climb without pressure. I usually like to focus on *how* I climb; I like to concentrate on making the movements as easy and beautiful as possible. This focus turns climbing into a sort of game for me, guiding me through the route so I can enjoy the process. When I enter in this state of flow, I am not thinking about anything: it's a very special feeling.

Another fundamental tool for climbers, directly related to concentration, is visualization. This involves imagining how I am going to feel executing a certain movement as if I were doing it at that exact moment. I focus on the way I take the holds, the position my body will assume to make the next move, but also on how I will *feel*.

I remember spending a lot of time in Oliana, Catalonia, visualizing my climbs from the ground below (the routes there are very long!). On my first 8c climb, called *Fish Eye*, my friend Anna asked me how my mental preparation had gone. Having visualized my movements, I already felt much more confident, proclaiming, 'Dude, I think I can climb this route'. And I did, completing the ascent

"Visualization ... involves imagining how I am going to feel executing a certain movement as if I were doing it at that exact moment. I focus on the way I take the holds, the position my body will assume to make the next move, but also on how I will *feel*."

← Over the Moon (5.12c)
Olivia Hsu contemplating her next moves to redpoint this ever-steepening route at Moon Hill near Yangshuo, China.

→ Mind Control (8c+)
Daila Ojeda paving the way on this 50m power-endurance test-piece, one of the most coveted of them all at Oliana, Catalunya, Spain.

later that day. I know it's important to mentally see myself climbing the routes, breathing properly when reaching the good resting holds, flowing and finally clipping the chain.

Personally, I find it difficult to stay focused in places where there is a lot of noise and information. For this reason, I like to climb long and more remote routes, like *Tom et Jerry* in the Gorges du Verdon or *Menhir* in the Dolomites, where I feel truly alone. Focus takes you to a state of total immersion where only the next move matters; without any distracting thoughts, you climb with confidence and control almost unconsciously.

Finding it easier to reach that famous state of flow when the outside environment is quiet might explain why I climb so badly in climbing gyms! If I'm attempting a route on a busy crag, it's crucial for me to cultivate a strong connection with my belayer to make sure that we are totally in tune – so I can climb without being distracted by any thoughts or fear of a fall. But if I know I'm not going to enjoy the experience because my attention is considerably reduced by crowds or noise, I might not even try a project – being distracted during a climb can also risk accident and injury.

Flow is also best achieved on a route that is physically possible but difficult enough to be challenging. Being a little intimidated by a route is actually a positive; it lowers my expectations so that I can focus on incremental progress instead of the end result. Sometimes I will even try routes when I don't know whether I'll be able to complete them.

When you've been training for an ascent and know each sequence, each movement, total concentration comes into play when you finally string them together to climb the entire route. At this point, you know that you can make it, but need long-term attention to do so. I like to create different strategies and divide the route into distinct phases, changing my focus as I go through them. A route is like a race – you have ups and downs and you have to learn to manage those moments, identify the feeding zones, put yourself in fight mode when necessary and then return to moments of calm.

Splitting the route into sections also allows me to anticipate obstacles. If I know that I am going to arrive exhausted at a rest point or that the crux will be very hard, I can come prepared. I like to be in control, so imagining these problems helps me brainstorm solutions in advance; all these internal conversations keep me focused and allow me to put the end goal from my mind.

It's important to have self-confidence to get through the highs and lows, and to keep believing in yourself no matter what. I need to channel positive thoughts to stay focused and like to remind

"Personally, I find it difficult to stay focused in places where there is a lot of noise and information. For this reason, I like to climb long and more remote routes, like *Tom et Jerry* in the Gorges du Verdon or *Menhir* in the Dolomites, where I feel truly alone."

← **Mind Control (8c+)**
Daila Ojeda in the zone on this aptly named route at Oliana, Catalunya, Spain.

"I began to think about how lucky I was just to be there. Letting go of the route and of my goal, memories came back to me – of how I started climbing in the Canary Islands – and I thought of where I was now, right here in Italy, doing what I loved most in life."

myself: 'You are where you wanted to be.' Too often we spend hours dreaming about a project and then fail to appreciate the moment.

And then sometimes, even with all the right training and strategies in place, you have to dig deep and find a bigger reason for completing a route. I'd had my sights on climbing *Menhir* in the Dolomites for some time, but my climbing partner only had one week to dedicate to the attempt. I was making progress, but on the last day I got discouraged and thought 'I can't climb this route. That's it.' Decision made, I sat down for a moment, just to relax and to take in the spectacular landscape around me. I began to think about how lucky I was just to be there. Letting go of the route and of my goal, memories came back to me – of how I started climbing in the Canary Islands – and I thought of where I was now, right here in Italy, doing what I loved most in life. That was enough – I went back to the wall, put on my climbing shoes and thought: 'Give yourself this attempt, climb for yourself, for your love of the sport.' And I completed the route with perfect focus.

→ Live the Life (28)
Garry Phillips gunning for the top of the final pitch of the mega route he established with Jake Bresnehan (belaying), on the massive conglomerate cliff above Lake Huntley in the Tyndall Range, deep in the wilderness of western Tasmania, Australia. Pitches are 21, 28, 27, 27, 26, 25.

FLOW

Inalee Jahn focused on the last moves of this fine route on the windswept crag of Wilyabrup, Margaret River region, Western Australia.

FLOW

← Aphelion (22)
Sabina Allemann calmly leading through the crux of the route, on the third of four pitches, on Mount Tibrogargan, Glass House Mountains, Queensland, Australia. Michael Hirning belaying.

→ Inespérance (7a)
Nadine Rousselot has some quick decisions to make as the next holds – pockets – are hard to see and the pump clock is ticking. This is pitch three of this steadily increasingly hard route (pitches are 6a+, 6b+, 6c+, 7a) on La Grand Face, Céüse, France. Monique Forestier belaying.

FLOW

A couple of classics out of the thousands of great
climbs that are largely hidden away in the forests
and hollows (enclosed valleys) of the Red River Gorge,
Kentucky, USA.

← Breakfast Burrito (5.10d)
Olivia Hsu casually warming up for the day
at Drive-By Crag.

→ Golden Boy (5.13b)
Leor Gold applying the right mix of power
and endurance for this popular hard route
at the Gold Coast.

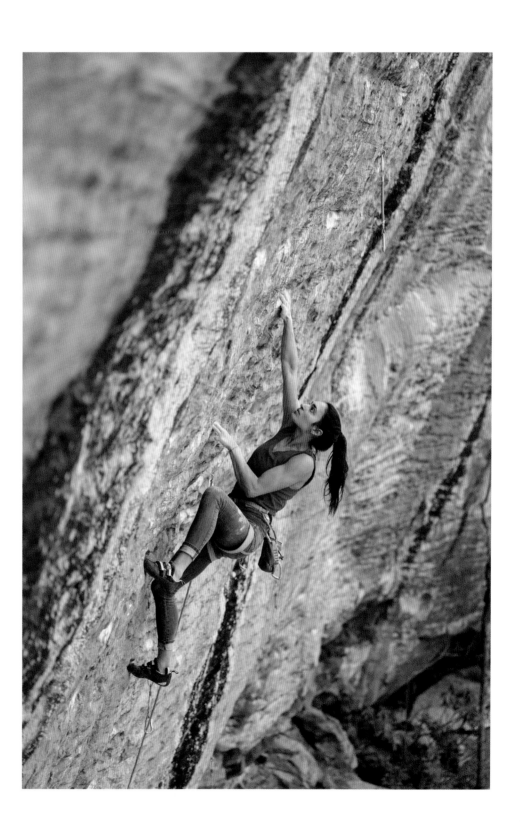

← Don't Wet Yourself (23)
Sarah Rose Williams, in this moment, perhaps a little
preoccupied with the crux moves of this atmospheric
route to notice Katooomba Falls in full-flow behind
her. It's in the Blue Mountains, NSW, Australia.
Jacques Beaudoin belaying.

→ Serpentine (29)
Lynn Hill concentrating on her successful ascent
of the 40m business pitch of this sensational
route, blasting up the middle of Taipan Wall, in the
Grampians, Victoria, Australia.

↓ The Free Route (25)
Lynn Hill keeping her eyes on the prize as she
nears the top of the Totem Pole – a 65m dolerite
column at Cape Hauy, Tasmania, Australia. Nancy
Feagin belaying.

↘ The Free Route (25)
Hazel Findlay engaged in her onsight of this variant
first pitch on the Totem Pole. This variant pitch, a more
popular later-day addition, is also known as the Deep
Play Variant (24) pitch.

↑ Tom et je Ris (8b+)
Monique Forestier a little extended as she slowly but
surely executes some of the last tricky moves on this
60m route in Verdon Gorge, France.

→ Tucán Ausente (7a)
Fred Moix no doubt fully attentive and appreciative
of the situation created by long run-outs combined
with ridiculous and not-entirely reliable blobby
conglomerate holds. This is the forth pitch of seven
on this premium 280m line on El Macizo del Pisón,
Riglos, Spain. Pitches are 6b+, 6b, 6b, 7a, 7c+, 7a, 6c.

These three images are from the highly engaging trad-climbing paradise on the limestone sea cliffs of Pembroke, Wales, UK.

← Herod (E1, 5b)
Charlie Woodburn perhaps looking for where he can plant his next bunch of protection in the garden at Mother Carey's Kitchen.

→ Fascist and Me (E3, 5C)
Steve Monks being somehow strangely baited, to the top of this two-pitch route, by Mike Weeks' tender toes.

↓ Sunlover Direct (E3, 5c)
Mike Weeks protecting his next upwardly mobile ambitions.

OVERHANGS

Text by Adam Ondra

Looking at overhanging rock from the ground feels very different to looking at a vertical wall. The rock could be just a section of a route that projects outwards; a roof that juts into space; the top of a cave; or an entire wall that is steeply overhanging. While vertical walls are often more aesthetic, overhangs have other attractions. They make climbing more adventurous, more crazy, more inaccessible to us as humans; instead, overhangs and caves are empires of birds, bats and spiders.

8

Vertical walls are often more pleasing to the eye than overhangs: sheer, almost blank-looking faces with just a couple of tiny edges, which might make a climb possible. You can certainly find huge blank overhangs too, but they are mostly impossible to scale. You need features to climb – even more so when you are in the middle of a massive cave or clinging to another kind of overhang. Yet the multiple promises of overhangs – including adventure and freedom – easily trump the aesthetics.

Příklepový Strop is an old aid-route in the Macocha Abyss, a huge sinkhole in the Moravian Karst cave system in the Czech Republic (or Czechia) that embodies the attraction of overhangs for me. For years, the Abyss had been left abandoned – without any attempts to free climb it – even though the route could have been considered the last great unresolved free-climbing problem in the country. It is undoubtedly the longest and steepest climb in Czechia at 180 metres (590 feet), with an overhang of 60 metres (197 feet). I harboured a strong desire to solve the puzzle, to free-climb the route that traversed such an iconic cliff.

Despite its appeal for me, *Příklepový Strop* might not seem like the most attractive route. The place is extremely damp – often too wet to climb. With access to the area only granted for a few days a year upon special request, you have to be lucky with the weather; a successful climb requires freezing conditions, otherwise condensation coats the rock. It also looks a bit chossy and dirty, and protection can be questionable. There are plenty of bolts, but they date from 1986, are only 2cm (0.8-inches) deep and, with the extreme humidity of the cave, they are heavily rusted. And while there are some pegs and a few newer bolts, several sections are quite run-out – with little or no protection – though there is the possibility of placing cams or nuts.

Czech climbers Dušan Janák (from my hometown of Brno) and Jan Straka started assessing *Příklepový Strop* for a potential free climb together in 2015 and in 2017. They could do all the moves, so the first step towards mastering this monster route was complete. However, the redpoint ascent felt too far away for them. I was extremely attracted to the idea of trying it, and even more by attempting to onsight it (completing the climb with no practice runs). But when I set off, with twenty quickdraws on my harness and a set of nuts and cams, it looked like the burden of the gear – on top of the weight of my expectations – might prove too heavy. The first pitch is 40 metres (131 feet) long and was a pure onsight – there was no sign of any chalk, just plenty of dirty rock and lots of question marks over where to place protection. I fell off after roughly 30 metres (98 feet), but it was an incredible fight – among the biggest of my life and paradoxically one of the feats of climbing I am proudest of.

"For years, the Abyss had been left abandoned – without any attempts to free climb it – even though the route could have been considered the last great unresolved free-climbing problem in the country."

⇇ Project
Ben Cossey getting frustratingly close to success on this short but super-powerful unclimbed open project, originally bolted by Jerry Moffat several decades earlier. It's on The Bluffs at Mount Arapiles, Victoria, Australia.

→ Los Revolucionarios (9a)
Adam Ondra bringing the grade of 9a to Greece for the first time (in 2009), with this first ascent of a steep project at Sector Odyssey on Kalymnos island.

OVERHANGS

"To my mind, that sense of freedom is also about knowing that it is okay to take a fall. Even a big fall. A steep overhang is one of the only places where, no matter how big the fall, you are safe."

Later on, I completed the pitch on my second try and the next day, free-climbed the entire route out into the rim of the chasm. Just a thirty-minute drive from my house, the whole thing was one of the best adventures I've ever had. The feeling of being insignificant, even unwanted, on this massive overhang, was huge. It felt odd to climb in the domain of bats and spiders. Of course, poor protection and chossy rock added spice and adventure, but climbing in this hole with almost no daylight was something special. I couldn't see the sky. Did that go against the whole idea of free climbing, which is tightly connected to the word 'freedom'? Can you really feel free when your eyes are staring into nothing but dark rock and spiderwebs?

I can think of a very different experience of cave climbing in Flatanger, Norway. The rock there is about as perfect as can be – flawlessly clean and solid – with an undeniable sense of freedom as you gaze across the beautiful watery Norwegian archipelago. Just as in Macocha, Flatanger has been the setting for some of the best climbing memories of my life. Climbing in a sea of the perfect granite before the setting sun, I felt just as free as in the deep dark cave back home, freezing in sub-zero temperatures. For me, feeling free is about climbing in the most improbable places imaginable: discovering blank spots on the map and marking them, if only with my fleeting presence. It is about knowing that I am capable of climbing up there – that I want to climb there, no matter how pointless it might seem to others. Big caves all over the world offer the same sense of uniqueness, freedom and wonder. There are no easy ways of rappelling into these spots – just like on the vertical walls.

To my mind, that sense of freedom is also about knowing that it is okay to take a fall. Even a big fall. A steep overhang is one of the only places where, no matter how big the fall, you are safe. There is nothing to hit (unless of course you actually land on the ground). That is probably the best bonus of climbing on an overhang, though it is often overlooked. Climbing should be about reaching higher, but also about taking falls, because that's the only way you can really progress. Those who don't fall, don't get better – or at least not at the same rate.

Climbing can be enjoyed no matter how steep the rock, or how scared you feel. Being scared and climbing through it, whether on sheer overhangs or in dark caverns, can bring about life's most memorable and life-affirming moments. Have no fear of fear. Sometimes fear is good.

← Jaws (8c)
Adam Ondra nicely navigating the stalactite-dripped roof of Sikati Cave for the flash of this 50m route on Kalymnos island, Greece.

← Milupa (28)
David Jones found the only real overhang on the Wall of Fools in the Grampians, Victoria, Australia.

← Divine Intervention (29 MO)
Monique Forestier working a featured roof on the underbelly of The Cathedral, high on the plateau of Mount Buffalo, Victoria, Australia.

↙ Mr Mean Goo (31)
Monique Forestier on a 25m route that tackles the proudest overhang at the hard sports crag of Diamond Falls, in the Blue Mountains, NSW, Australia.

↓ Superstyling (25)
Monique Forestier getting some Pacific Ocean views at Point Perpendicular, NSW, Australia.

→ **Ghetto Superstar (28)**
Sean Powell slogging along this 22m roof climb at
The Hideaway, a surprising later-day discovery in the
bushlands of suburban Sydney, Australia.

OVERHANGS

↓ Burnt Offerings (7a+)
Monique Forestier relishing steep rock and shade in
this little cave, with a good view of Ton Sai, Thailand.

→ Le Denti (7c+)
Chloé Minoret squeezing in a last burn for the
day in this large cave at Goudes, overlooking the
Mediterranean, Les Calanques, France.

OVERHANGS

Passport to Insanity (27)
The 6m downward-sloping roof with a crack running
through it, on the second pitch, is the highlight
(and crux) of this crazy three-pitch trad climb on
The Fortress in the Grampians, Victoria, Australia.

← Jill McLeod turning the lip of the roof with Kirsty
Hamilton belaying.

↗ Malcolm Matheson at the end of the 6m roof.

↑ **Gutbuster (5.14c)**
Jason Campbell found the most overhanging line out
of the Souls Cave for this test-piece of his at Mount
Charleston, near Las Vegas, Nevada, USA.

↗ **Space Odyssey (27)**
Nathan Hoette coming to the end of his journey on
this jutting prow, the second of two pitches at The
Lost World in the Grampians, Victoria, Australia.

→ **Great Divide (28)**
Jacques Beaudoin on this ever-steepening thin trad
crack that he discovered, inside the Disbelief Cave on
the Newnes Plateau, Blue Mountains, NSW, Australia.
Dave Dave belaying.

↘ **Double Adapter (31)**
Roman Hofmann traversing the lip of a cave at
Gateway in the Blue Mountains, NSW, Australia.

→ Priapos (7c)
Evan Stevens finding his way through the confusing
curtain of stalactites on this mightily overhanging
40m route in the Grande Grotta, Kalymnos, Greece.

OVERHANGS

↑ **Typhoon (7c+)**
Olivier Michellod leading this 40m climb – so long and overhanging that it requires a 100m rope to lower-off at the end. It's in Crystal Cave, on Telendos Island near Kalymnos, Greece. Simon Montmory belaying.

↗ **Tantrum (8b)**
Grant Rowbottom impressing patrons of the nearby beach bar with his successful efforts on this slippery ceiling at Tonsai, Thailand.

→ **Clocks (22)**
Catherine Destivelle leading this once-popular overhang at Balls Head, with Sydney city in the background, NSW, Australia.

AQUATIC

Text by Tim Emmett

Climbing above or near the ocean holds a particular appeal to climbers. It's not just that sea cliffs provide high-quality climbing – there's also something about the presence of the ocean, or any water, that can affect our psyche in interesting ways. Pounding waves can induce a gut-wrenching fear, especially when they get too close. Tranquil seas and a beautiful beach nearby can make for a fun and wholesome time out. Then, sometimes, the ocean allows us to forego the use of ropes, when the sea itself becomes our crash mat and we can climb with total freedom.

9

> "For me, deep-water soloing is the purest form of climbing: there's no gear, no protection, no ropes, no extra weight."

As I got closer to the edge, I could feel my heart pounding against my chest. I had no idea that what I was about to see was the foundation of a new sport, one that would attract climbers hungry for adventure from around the world. I crouched down, and then onto my knees, carefully placing my hands on the edge of the cliff. I lowered my body down and forwards so I could peer over, without losing my balance and falling off.

I couldn't believe my eyes – the overhanging wall was *high*. The rock looked pristine, with a distinct contrast between shades of grey and orange, more like the stripes from a tiger's back. At 18–21 metres (60 or 70 feet), my mind went into overdrive, contemplating what a fall might be like from the top. Climbing on a cliff like this, with no safety rope or protection, other than the water below, took me back to my BASE-jumping years. I knew that 20 metres (65 feet) was exactly two seconds of free fall.

That might not seem like much, but two seconds when you're in the air can feel like eternity. Just think about the last time you went bouldering and fell off a highball. Or imagine climbing out the window of a six-storey building.

There is water below you. You do a hard move to get the next hold but miss. You're falling ... and you're falling ... you're still falling ... then splash, you land in the water! Refreshed and exhilarated, you swim to the surface where you open your mouth and fill your lungs with air, then look up to where you've just departed from.

Whenever I climb by the sea I am energized by the raw energy of the ocean, but the sea also provides a safe landing, which makes deep-water soloing possible. For me, deep-water soloing is the purest form of climbing: there's no gear, no protection, no ropes, no extra weight. It's much like bouldering: you string a sequence of moves together, without stopping. Stack multiple boulder problems on top of each other, with a giant bouldering mat below – the water – and you start to get the idea, dialling up the excitement factor by going higher and higher.

With deep-water soloing, you don't have to interrupt the flow of climbing to clip a bolt or place protection. All you do is get the next hold, pull on it, look for another and keep going. The sense of excitement grows the higher you get: the further you are from the water, the greater the consequences of a misjudged landing. Sometimes the top is tantalizingly close – yet so far away when you are in extremis, arms full of lactic acid, fingers uncurling, even from the largest holds. The tension between approaching the ascent at the same time as contemplating a rapid descent to the waters below is enthralling, and creates a magical moment where you either unleash an all-out attack for the top – or take to the air. Much to the amusement of those watching from above.

← Liquid Insanity (23)
Robyn Cleland focusing on things other than the churning cauldron below this arête at Point Perpendicular, NSW, Australia.

→ The Shrubbery (7c+)
Tim Emmett took a couple of splashes before succeeding on this deep-water solo that he found on the 12m-high Holy Grail Wall, Mana Island, near Kornati, Croatia.

AQUATIC

"Like ghosts, [waves] arrive in sets every twenty or thirty minutes, so a relatively calm sea can quickly be transformed into a frothing cauldron of water with little or no warning."

I remember climbing in Croatia on the Kornati islands, spending long days and nights on a boat with friends. Sailing around looking for the ultimate rock climb, never touched by human hands. Armed only with shoes, shorts and a chalk bag, we sought cliffs with striking features that inspired us to climb on them. Living on the ocean, going into the unknown, is a true form of adventure.

Whether deep-water soloing or traditional climbing, being by the sea provides a unique experience. Not only are you surrounded by infinite space, but the environment can also be very dynamic and full of energy. Strong winds cause large waves that can explode on impact when they hit the base of the land; spray can soak you even when you're at the top of a 30-metre (100ft) cliff. Surrounded by the ocean, there's usually no way out of a climb except by reaching the top. This adds an extra element of adventure, especially if you are ambitious and attempt a climb at your limit. Success is not guaranteed.

Traditional climbing on a cliff like Gogarth, in North Wales, is a particularly cerebral experience because, apart from all the other thrills, the rock can be as soft as mud. Quartz juts out of the soft rock the only thing solid enough to pull on or wrap a sling around, more for psychological reassurance than anything else.

On exposed cliffs, the largest and most powerful waves come from thousands of miles away. Like ghosts, they arrive in sets every twenty or thirty minutes, so a relatively calm sea can quickly be transformed into a frothing cauldron of water with little or no warning. Tides can also sweep in, creating rapid and extreme changes in water level. Climbing in this environment is not for the faint hearted; it takes a particular type of person to experience nature's unpredictability as truly exciting.

Climbing by the water also means sharing the environment with its inhabitants. There are often birds, especially on the more remote sea cliffs like those found in Scotland. Seagulls are one thing but watch out for fulmars at all costs. Their main form of defence is to regurgitate a disgusting fluid from their gut, which they spit with devastating accuracy and surprising range. The result is a viscous sticky liquid attack – so putrid that it churns the stomach.

Sea-cliff climbing on islands is perhaps the most adventurous of all; sometimes you have to swim to get to a sea stack. Often no one knows you're there, isolated from the human world, apart from the wildlife that surrounds you.

The physical presence of the ocean – the crashing waves, squawking seabirds, the salty sea spray and the dancing sun on its surface – adds another dimension to the climbing experience. It also opens up two of my favourite climbing styles: deep-water soloing and sea-cliff climbing, where energy, freedom and uncertainty make for an intoxicating mix.

← The Gateaux Thief (E6 6b)
Tim Emmett making the first ascent of this deep-water solo which, at 18m, is too high for comfort and has been rarely – if ever – repeated. It's at Stennis Ford, Pembroke, Wales, UK.

AQUATIC

← Free Born Man (E4 6a)
Dave Pickford climbing this popular, tall (17m-high), deep-water solo at Conner Cove, Swanage, Dorset, UK.

→ Davy Jones's Locker (E4 6a)
Dave Pickford not too perturbed that the rough swell would make any fall from this long traversing deep-water solo more serious than usual. It's at Conner Cove, Dorset, UK.

↓ Project
Leo Houlding making a massive dynamic move, but not quite snagging the next hold, on this deep-water solo – thus he'll momentarily be taking a dip in the Adriatic Sea again. It's on Panitula Island, near Kornati, Croatia.

AQUATIC

← Choy Sum (23)
Lee Cossey climbing above a lively sea at Popeye Wall, Point Perpendicular, NSW, Australia. Ben Cossey belaying.

← Turtle Cave (7a+)
Monique Forestier pondering her options having reached her objective for this deep-water solo. The route traversed in from the left side of the image, then down the stalactite, until approximately 10m above the ocean at Halong Bay, Vietnam.

↘ The Diving Board (7a+)
Lee Cujes now only has to somehow mantle onto this cool feature for the full tick. It's at Unemployment Wall, Halong Bay, Vietnam.

↑ River Rage (27)
Jason Piper, prior to his successful first ascent, on this high (15+m) deep-water solo at Crafty's on the Hawkesbury River near Sydney, NSW, Australia.

→ Prowess (23)
Amanda Morrissey on the Sydney sea cliffs at Bow Wall in Vaucluse, Sydney, Australia.

← Southern Ocean Swell (12)
Ali Chapman leading, with Ashlee Peeters belaying,
the second pitch of this two-pitch trad route on the
Southern Ocean Wall. As the names hint, this wall is
notorious for being smashed by enormous waves. It's
at West Cape Howe, Western Australia.

↑ Friendless Variant (17)
Chris Kavazos leading, with Ashlee Peeters belaying,
another atmospheric route on the dolerite cliffs of
West Cape Howe, Western Australia.

→ La Commune (6b)
Nadine Rousselot leading the final – and exit – pitch
of this unusual nine-pitch traverse route at Les
Calanques, on the Mediterranean in the south of
France. The route actually starts from the rocky
'beach' in the background!

↑ **Travels with my Aunt (6a)**
Rachel Carr grateful not to be bothered by wild
monkeys on the beach (like the day before), at
Hin Tak Wall, Koh Phi Phi Island, Thailand.

→ **Look to the West (28)**
Jack Folkes making one of his countless ground-up
attempts, made in forty-four sessions spread over
two-and-a-half years, prior to succeeding on the
first ascent of this tricky deep-water solo on the
Shoalhaven River near Nowra, NSW, Australia.

← **The Fear (19)**
The presence of the ocean is one of the factors that make this two-pitch climb more terrifying than most; imperfect protection, sandy rock and the crazy setting on the North Head of Sydney Harbour, in Australia, are others. Chris Firth walking the plank with Chris Diemont belaying.

↗ **Smoked Bananas (17)**
Who knows, this technique might catch on? Dave James utilizing a double-fist and head jam on this wide line at Frog Buttress, Queensland, Australia.

233

PHOTO NOTES
by Simon Carter

CLIMBING KIT

My kit for photography differs from my normal climbing kit in a few ways. When fixing a rope, I prefer a static rather than a dynamic rope; they stretch less, making it easier to use ascenders and better able to withstand damage. Even with a static rope, I use rope protectors and re-belay (tie off) my rope below sharp sections. Ascenders are essential for freeing my hands to use the camera and for sprinting to a new position higher up the rope.

In addition to my normal climbing harness, I find a chest harness essential for my photography. A chest harness makes hanging on a rope more comfortable and enables me to lean out from the cliff for a better perspective on the climb. Being comfortable enables me to concentrate on operating the camera, precisely frame the shot and hold that position for a long time. A chest harness is lighter, more versatile and is faster to work with than, say, a 'bosun's chair' – though that might be a good option for shooting video and/or if you're going to be stuck in one position for a long time.

- Static rope. Often a 60m (197ft) length is used, but whatever the situation requires.

- Comfortable climbing harness.

- Chest harness. Comfortable and functional chest harnesses are hard to find, but invaluable.

- Climbing rack. Quickdraws, locking carabiners and slings. Traditional protection (cams and wires) may be useful, or required, depending on the situation.

- Ascenders.

- Abseil device.

- Rope hook. Helps with rope management and for quickly pulling your abseil rope up and out of the shot.

- Extra camming device. For tensioning to a second rope.

- Rope protectors.

- Helmet. Used when there is a danger of rockfall.

→ **A Girl's Best Friend (24)**
Douglas Bell ripping – and nearly riding – an enormous roof flake off this sport route at Lasseter's, Nowra, NSW, Australia. Fortunately, the flake missed his belayer and Doug was pretty much unscathed.

If much of the appeal of climbing comes from the physical feat and the art of problem-solving in beautiful natural surroundings, then taking photographs on the rock face adds a whole other dimension. Capturing an arresting shot means looking for the perfect frame and making the most of dramatic natural features for maximum graphic impact. The challenge is getting you – and your equipment – into exactly the right spot at the right time, sometimes dangling in precarious positions.

I believe it's important to have a strong concept for a shot and to be prepared; planning and preparation puts the odds in your favour. But not everything can be predicted or guaranteed in climbing photography, so it's also crucial to be spontaneous and seize an opportunity should it arise.

A key question I ask myself is, 'What is unique about this particular climb or place – and how do I emphasize that?' There might be something about the rock architecture, the setting or the climber, that could be interesting to accentuate in the shot. The answer often results in a strong concept for a photograph, which then provides goals for where the photographer (and climbers) should ideally be – and when.

My methods depend on the situation, what I've envisaged for the shot and how familiar I am with the area. I might spend days getting to know a new place, perhaps climbing some routes, looking around for interesting climbs, noticing what the light is doing at different times of day, abseiling down in different spots and seeing what angles I can find; what compositions I might be able to create. In the Blue Mountains, for instance, I wanted to capture the majesty of the 'inversion layer' of clouds that sometimes sits in the valleys at dawn. I eventually found a climb on a long-forgotten cliff line that was nicely situated and caught the dawn light. It then took three aborted pre-dawn starts before one day the cloud was sufficiently thick and everything came together (see the result on pages 76–77).

Inevitably, the main challenge in climbing photography is physically getting into the right place to 'get an angle' on the action and the setting to achieve the shot you want. Sometimes this is straightforward, such as when an easy hike to the base of the cliff – or the cliff top – gives a good angle. Perhaps a little scrambling will provide a vantage point. However, often the only way to get the right shot is from a fixed (anchored) rope, which is how most of the images in this book were taken.

The difficulty of rigging a rope depends entirely on the surroundings. I may have to climb up a route to anchor my rope, which I can sometimes do, but often the climber-cum-model will do it for me; I've always appreciated a good 'rope gun'. In other situations, I can hike or scramble to the cliff top and fix the rope from above. Once a rope is safely fixed, it is a simple process of abseiling down or using 'ascenders' attached to the rope to climb up, as desired.

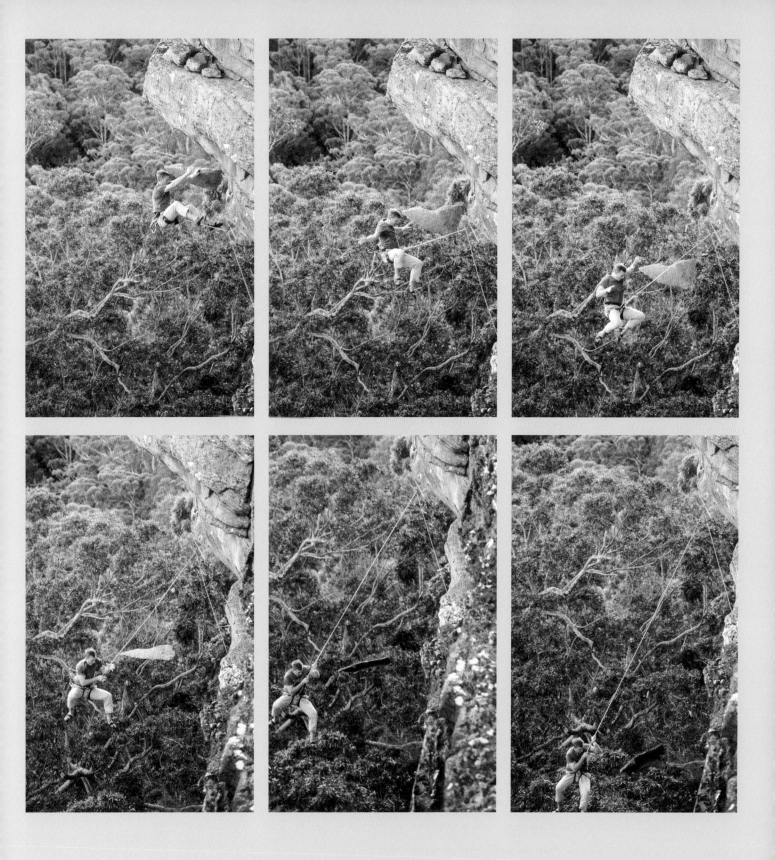

↖ Simon Carter at work photographing the first ascent of the West Peak of Mount Huashan, China. See photo pp. 6–7 and 251.

← Simon Carter using his 'Photo Pole' apparatus at Frog Buttress, Queensland, Australia.

↙ Simon Carter using his 'Photo Frame' at Hanging Rock in the Blue Mountains, NSW, Australia.

There are a few tricks for working effectively from a fixed rope. A major challenge occurs when the climb is overhanging, and thus the rope is dangling in space with nothing to stop the photographer from spinning around uncontrollably. You have to be somehow tethered to a second rope to stop the spin – although you may not need a second rope if the tail-end of the main rope will do. The solution is to attach the rope to something – such as an anchor point (often a bolt) on a climb, a tree out from the base of the cliff or a cliff top – anything so you can tension on a second rope to stop the spinning and better control your position. Taking this further, using two ropes strung between different spots might enable you to tension out into a favourable position that provides a unique perspective. A good example of this is the image on page 19, where I was attached to one rope fixed to the summit of the Totem Pole, then tensioned out away from the pillar with a second rope attached to the mainland some 40 metres (131 feet) behind me.

There's no doubt that often getting a bit 'out' from the cliff will improve the perspective and show more of the climb or situation. So, a greater challenge in climbing photography occurs when there is no anchor point, or opposite cliff line, to attach a second rope to – as is common on bigger cliffs. There's nothing there, just space, so how will you get yourself, or at least the camera, out from the cliff for a better angle?

I started dabbling around with possible solutions to this problem in 1996 when I designed an A-frame apparatus, which I dubbed the 'Photo Frame', and had it welded together by an aluminium fabrication company. While the Photo Frame provided some unique and otherwise impossible angles, it was cumbersome to set up and lacked versatility as it was pretty much fixed in position.

In 2006, when I was in the Red River Gorge, Kentucky, USA, inspired by the autumn colours, I decided to play around with an evolution of the concept. I realized to get the camera out from the cliff didn't mean that I had to get out there as well physically. So, I rigged an 8-metre (26-foot) long painter's pole out from the cliff, with the camera hanging off the end. A video feed from the camera to a little monitor showed how I needed to adjust the camera position and framing, and a remote trigger was used to fire the shutter. I called this my 'Photo Pole' apparatus. Over the years, I refined the rigging, so that I could pull the camera up to me without moving my position. I used this setup to capture some unique images, such as the Devil's Tower photographs on pages 116 and 117.

Camera technology continues to change and evolve. It certainly makes some shots easier or even possible in a way they weren't before, and there are plenty of ways technology can be, and is, creatively implemented in climbing photography. Yet I'm surprised how little things have changed over the years. That's because the

SAFETY

'Personal responsibility' is a fundamental concept in climbing. Taking responsibility for our decisions and actions, rather than blaming external factors, ultimately helps keep us safe. The notion can seem harsh but it's also quite liberating; without it, the sport wouldn't really exist.

Personal responsibility is also important for photographers. And because photographers on the rock face might influence what climbers do, it's crucial to be fully aware of the interaction and the risks being taken. The issue of soloing – climbing without ropes – is the obvious one to consider, but there are plenty of other dangerous situations that can also occur. Climbing photographers would never want to cause or contribute to an accident, so thinking carefully about one's influence on events is a moral imperative.

My advice to aspiring climbing photographers is to get some years of solid climbing experience before trying to add photography into the equation. I'm very grateful for the ten years of diverse climbing I'd done before getting serious with the camera. It's not about becoming a better or 'harder' climber, it's about gaining the skills and experience. It's about rope work and rigging, which make you safer and more productive. It's also about understanding what is happening around you at the crag and what the climbers are going through.

Mixing photography with climbing adds extra complications, as there is more to go wrong. Scrambling unroped around cliff tops and across ledges, especially with equipment, is dangerous. The risk of dislodging rocks, or anything else, onto climbers below, is one photographers should be acutely aware of. There are many mistakes and misjudgments that you can make. Complacency, bravado and haste can exacerbate potential problems. Take it easy out there.

fundamental challenge, that of being in the right place at the right time, is just as important as it ever was.

Of course, it may well be foolish to predict the future. Drones are increasingly appearing on the scene, not just for video, for which they have long been invaluable, but for still photographs as well. The technology and quality keep evolving so that it is now possible to take close-in, even vertically framed, high-quality images from drones. Of course, there will always be places where it is not legal or desirable to use drones, and where they will be outright annoying (or worse!) for climbers – especially when attempting to get close up on the action. So, while I don't want to speculate, I doubt drones will be a silver bullet for saving huge amounts of work in all situations. Suffice it to say, drones were not used for any of the images in this book. Style is important in climbing. Maybe it's important for climbing photography too?

GLOSSARY

ABSEIL aka RAPPEL Method for sliding down a rope.

AID CLIMBING Mechanically assisted climbing. Body weight is supported by protection, or other equipment, and used to directly 'aid' upwards progress. An 'aid route' is a route that is ascended using aid climbing.

ARÊTE A sharp edge of rock jutting out from the main cliff face, like an outside corner of a building.

ASCENDERS Mechanical devices used for ascending a rope. They slide up but they have a cam so that they don't slide down.

BELAY The system using a rope to arrest a climber's fall. Includes the anchors and/or protection points and involves using a friction (belay) device to lock off the rope.

BELAYER The person using the rope to provide safety to the person climbing.

BETA Usually the sequence of movements required to climb a section of rock. To tell someone 'beta' is to give advice – either about movements or other insight for a particular route. 'Micro beta' is when the movements required are subtle.

BIG WALL A big cliff face offering particularly long routes, possibly requiring numerous days to climb.

BOLT A bolt fixed into a pre-drilled hole, used as a permanent anchor or protection point.

BOULDERING Unroped climbing, close to the ground. Mats or bouldering 'pads' are usually placed on the ground to soften falls.

CAM A camming device. A type of climbing hardware that is used for protection, cams are placed into cracks and expand to lock into place.

CARABINER aka BINER An essential piece of hardware: exceptionally strong metal alloy snaplinks, used to connect climbers, ropes and protection in various ways.

CHOSS, CHOSSY Soft, loose and crumbly – basically low-quality rock.

CRAG A smaller cliff or set of cliffs.

CRANK To pull hard on a handhold.

CRIMP A small handhold, allowing fingertips only.

CRUX The most difficult section of the climb.

DEADPOINT A fast 'dynamic' movement where the next handhold is grabbed at the moment the apex of upwards movement is reached.

DEEP-WATER SOLOING (DWS) Climbing without a rope or protection above deep water, usually the ocean.

EDGE Small handhold. In the UK, it is also the name given to some small outcrops of rock.

EXPOSED Being a long way above the ground, often resulting in an enhanced feeling of nervousness.

FACE A steep open section of cliff.

FLASH To lead climb a route on the very first attempt but with some prior knowledge of the difficulties or sequence of moves.

FREE CLIMBING Using hands and feet (and any other body part) to climb the rock's natural features. The rope and protection are there but not weighted or used to directly 'aid' the ascent.

GRADE A subjective rating of the difficulty of a climb. There are different grading systems for aid climbs, free climbs and boulder problems. See the international grading table on page 241 to convert between the most used free-climbing grading scales.

GROUND-UP To climb from ground level without previous inspection or preparation from above (such as from abseil).

HIGHBALL High bouldering. Climbing unroped on boulders, going so high that a fall will likely be nasty.

JAM, JAMMING OR JAMBING A climbing technique where a hand, foot or other body part is squeezed inside a crack to provide a hold.

JUG A very large hold.

LAYBACK, LAYBACKING A technique where you pull on – or lean off – a crack or edge with your hands, while your feet push against the wall, to provide an opposing force.

LEADER The first person of a party climbing a route. The leader clips the rope into protection points along the way while belayed from below.

LOCKING OFF Pulling up and holding on to the rock with your arm in a bent position, so you're steady and can move your other arm.

MESA An isolated, flat-topped mountain, surrounded by cliff line on all sides. 'Tepui' is a South American name for a mesa.

MICRO BETA See Beta.

MULTI-PITCH A longer route which has more than a single pitch of climbing.

OFFWIDTH A wide crack, awkward to climb.

ONSIGHT To lead climb a route making a successful ascent on the first attempt. The climber has no prior knowledge of the specific difficulties of the route. This is widely considered the best lead-climbing style.

OVERHANG An extra steep (overhanging) section of rock.

PITCH The section of climbing between two belays, not longer than the length of the rope.

PITON A metal wedge that is hammered into small cracks in the rock and used as protection.

PORTALEDGE A portable ledge! Made from alloy and fabric, climbers assemble these ledges on big cliffs when needed for belaying or camping. With a fly covering, they are like tents for cliffs.

PROJECT A climb which has been attempted but not yet properly free-climbed. To 'project' a route

(or 'projecting') is to attempt and practise a climb on multiple days with the aim of ultimately free climbing the route.

PROTECTION, PRO Various types of equipment placed in rock features to stop a falling climber. Natural or traditional protection is removable (non-permanent). Fixed protection is anchor points permanently fixed in the rock (including bolts or pitons).

PUMPY Strenuous climbing. A 'pump' is the lactic acid build-up that you get from strenuous climbing; a tiredness mostly felt in the forearms.

QUICKDRAW aka DRAW Two carabiners joined by a short strong nylon sling. Used to connect the rope to protection points.

RAPPEL See Abseil.

REDPOINT A style of climbing, widely regarded as the minimum standard for a 'free' ascent. The route must be led without a fall or any assistance from the rope or protection.

ROOF A horizontal, or near horizontal, overhanging section of rock.

ROPE GUN An experienced climber who can climb up difficult routes and set up ropes for others.

ROUTE The planned path, or direction, that a climb takes. Routes are usually named and graded.

RUN-OUT The distance the lead climber is above their last piece of protection. A run-out climb has big fall potential.

SECOND The climber who ascends a route or pitch after the lead climber. They are belayed from above.

SLAB A large off-vertical span of rock: seemingly featureless, it is often climbed with balance and friction techniques.

SLOPER A rounded smooth hold gripped with an open hand.

SOLO To climb alone. In free climbing, this means without a rope (free solo). In aid climbing, a rope is used (aid solo).

SPORT CLIMBING Where permanent fixed protection (commonly bolts) is utilized thereby allowing for an emphasis on gymnastic movement.

TEST-PIECE A climb, usually iconic, which is a standard of difficulty, or benchmark, for its grade.

TOP-ROPE To climb with the rope belayed or anchored from above.

TRADITIONAL CLIMBING aka TRAD Climbing characterized by the placing of temporary removable protection (slings, nuts, camming devices).

TRAVERSE To climb sideways, horizontally.

TUFA A fin-like rock formation found in limestone.

TYROLEAN TRAVERSE To slide along a rope fixed between two formations that are elevated and separated by a void.

GRADING TABLE

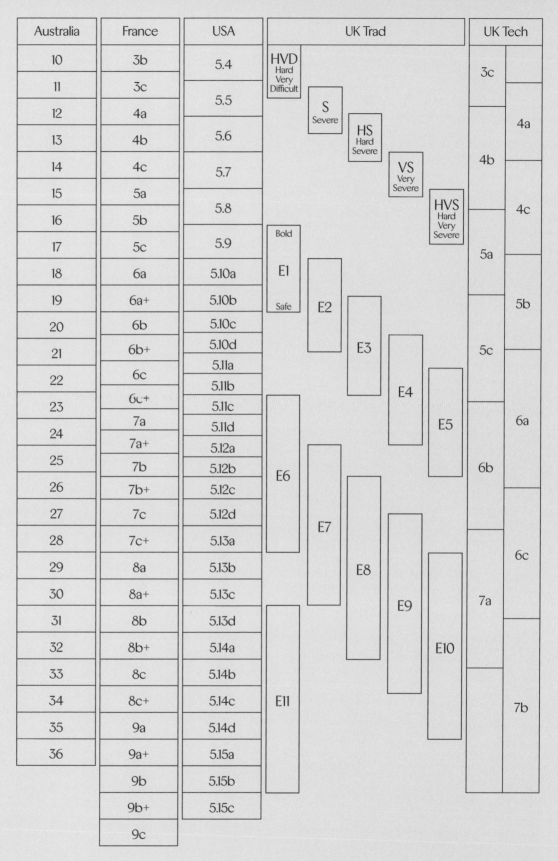

Australia	France	USA	UK Trad					UK Tech	
10	3b	5.4	HVD Hard Very Difficult					3c	
11	3c	5.5							4a
12	4a			S Severe					
13	4b	5.6			HS Hard Severe			4b	
14	4c	5.7				VS Very Severe			4c
15	5a						HVS Hard Very Severe		
16	5b	5.8						5a	
17	5c	5.9	Bold E1 Safe						5b
18	6a	5.10a		E2					
19	6a+	5.10b						5c	
20	6b	5.10c			E3				
21	6b+	5.10d				E4			6a
22	6c	5.11a					E5	6b	
		5.11b							
23	6c+	5.11c	E6						
24	7a	5.11d			E7				
	7a+	5.12a				E8			
25	7b	5.12b							
26	7b+	5.12c					E9		6c
27	7c	5.12d						7a	
28	7c+	5.13a					E10		
29	8a	5.13b							
30	8a+	5.13c							
31	8b	5.13d	E11						7b
32	8b+	5.14a							
33	8c	5.14b							
34	8c+	5.14c							
35	9a	5.14d							
36	9a+	5.15a							
	9b	5.15b							
	9b+	5.15c							
	9c								

SELECTED ROUTES
#01   THE NORTHERN CELESTIAL MASTERS (5.12+ or E6)

Leo Houlding during the ground-up first ascent of their 600-metre (1,968-foot) fourteen-pitch route, established with Wang Zhi Ming and Carlos Suarez, on the West Peak of Mount Huashan, China. See photo, pages 6–7.

This mini-expedition aimed to scale the as-yet-unclimbed main face on the West Peak of the mountain. We had a few days to scope things out, in which Leo and his partners decided to attempt to free climb up the vegetation-covered arête of the mountain, rather than the steeper, cleaner wall to the left, which would have required much aiding. I needed to abseil in from above, so for me, the tricky part was finding and anticipating where the route might top out. I was blessed to have a porter carry a load of my gear up the hundreds of steps carved into this sacred mountain. The next day they succeeded on the climb, despite the rain, and I was in position and got the shots.

SELECTED ROUTES
#02 POLE DANCER (22)

Steve Moon climbing a pillar at the very end of Cape Raoul on the Tasman Peninsula, Tasmania, Australia. See photo, page 32.

 The approach to the pillars at the end of Cape Raoul is long and complicated. To maximize our time out there, our party of four started by making the 7-kilometre (4-mile) hike out to the cliffs in the afternoon, where we found a place to camp out in the open. At dawn the next day we started with a 25-metre (82-foot) abseil, then a twenty-minute walk across a huge ledge. Next, we climbed a two-pitch grade 18 trad route to the top of the large 'Wedding Cake' formation, walked across that and abseiled 25 metres (82 feet) off the far side. Some scrambling then led to another abseil down slabby ledges to reach the start of the *Pole Dancer* route. To get the photo, I just had to hang back at a vantage point while climbers Steve and Monique continued on and scaled the route. To get out, we had to reverse everything: climbing up the abseil ropes that we had left in place; abseiling where we had climbed up. We got back to the cars well after dark.

SELECTED ROUTES
#03 MANARA-POTSINY (8a)

Toni Lamprecht on pitch eight of this 600-metre (1,968-foot) route on Tsaranoro Be, Tsaranoro, Madagascar. See photo, pages 86–87. (The photo on page 1 is also from this route, taken on another day.)

We left camp at around 4 a.m. so that we could do the hour-long hike to the route and climb up fixed ropes to this pitch – the eighth pitch of the climb – in time for dawn. I was delighted to see that an inversion layer of cloud had formed in the valley behind, a phenomenon that I knew occurred there from time to time but could not predict with the limited weather forecast available. The cloud dissipated quickly but I was also able to get some shots of Felix Frieder and Benno Wagner, who were helping Toni establish this route 'ground-up' in typical Tsaranoro style.

SELECTED ROUTES
#04 OZYMANDIAS DIRECT (28)

Steve Monks leading pitch two of the nine-pitch route that he freed on the North Wall, Mount Buffalo, Victoria, Australia. See photo, page 108.

This photo was taken a long way down this 270-metre (886-foot) route. The quickest approach to get Steve and his belayer to the start of the second pitch, so that he could re-lead it for the camera, was to fix static ropes all the way down to this point, perhaps 240 metres (787 feet). That also gave me a rope to work from for the photographs. Fortunately, it's only a ten-minute hike to the top of the route, and Steve's familiarity with it helped with the rigging. It was a lot of rope for us to climb up, and then haul up, afterwards though.

SELECTED ROUTES
#05 TOM ET JE RIS (8b+)

Monique Forestier on a 60-metre (197-foot) tufa route in the Verdon Gorge, France. See photo, page 115.

This route is approached by an hour-and-twenty minute hike, then abseiling down the 60-metre (197-foot) route. After several days of attempts, Monique succeeded in climbing the route, and so a few days later we returned with a belayer and she re-climbed the route in sections so that I could shoot both stills and video. I worked from the abseil rope and, as the route is overhanging and I was dangling in space, I needed to clip the tail end of the rope to bolts higher up on the route so that I was stable for shooting and filming.

SELECTED ROUTES
#06   MR CLEAN (5.11a)

Brittany Griffith on one of the immaculate lines on Devil's Tower, Wyoming, USA. See photo, page 116.

I first photographed Lisa Gnade on this route several years earlier, but I was not entirely happy with the result; it didn't really show how extraordinary the hexagonal columns are. The thought that I really needed to get the camera somewhere 'out there', away from the wall, stayed with me for years and led to the development of my 'Photo Pole' apparatus. It was satisfying to return years later, assemble the apparatus with an 8-metre (26-foot) painter's pole, haul it up the rope Brittney had set up for me and get the shot – despite the wind nearly (though thankfully not) ripping the pole from my grip and smashing my Nikon D3s into the rock.

SELECTED ROUTES
#07   PROJECT

Chris Sharma attempting pitch four of his 250-metre (820-foot) project at Mont-rebei, Spain. Tentative pitch grades are 6c+, 9a, 8b, 8c, 8c, 7b, 8c+. See photo, page 143.

Chris had established this route ground-up and had been working on it over several years. When it's freed, it will be one of the hardest multi-pitch routes in the world. The approach is a one-hour-and-fifteen minute hike – and then you have to cross the river, a feat achieved using an inflatable raft that we'd carried. As Chris and Klemen Bečan were working various pitches, all I had to do to get the shots was to use ascenders to climb the fixed ropes that they already had in place. It was getting dark by the time we got to pitch four, but high ISO on a digital camera enabled me to get this shot. Then we just had to abseil down, then raft and hike out in the dark.

SELECTED ROUTES
#08 ZODIAC (A2 5.7 or 5.13d)

Alex Huber in the midst of setting an El Capitan speed record of two hours, 31 minutes and 20 seconds on this 600-metre (1,968-foot) route in Yosemite, California, USA. See photo, page 149.

     To first get to the top of El Capitan, I used ascenders to climb up four fixed ropes – of questionable quality – that were on the East Ledges descent route and hiked to the top. Then, to get into position, I abseiled 60 metres (196 feet) down from the top. Knowing when Alex and Thomas Huber planned to start climbing, and how quick they might be, I knew I had an hour before they would likely come into view. I used this time to compose some shots and plan for when to change lenses (so I could get both scene setters and closer in action), and when I might need to sprint up the rope to a high position. In the end, it all happened faster than I could have possibly imagined.

SELECTED ROUTES
#09 SERPENTINE (29)

Lynn Hill leading the business pitch of this iconic route up the highest part of Taipan Wall, Grampians, Victoria, Australia. See photo, page 184.

This photo was taken from an abseil rope while Lynn was going for it on her redpoint. So, it was mainly a matter of having to decide on when to concentrate on shooting (and changing film, as this was captured on film) and when to quickly ascend my fixed rope to a higher position as Lynn climbed. Getting my 65-metre (213-foot) static rope, climbing gear for rigging and camera gear to the top of the route in the first place was done by climbing a grade 8 access route at the left end of Taipan Wall, then walking and scrambling – much of it exposed – around to the top of *Serpentine* to set up.

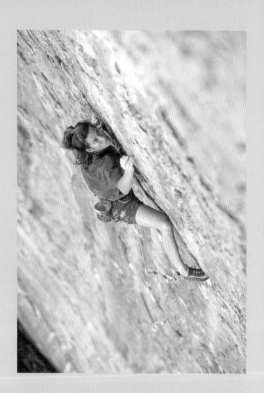

SELECTED ROUTES
#10 TUCÁN AUSENTE (7a)

Fred Moix leading pitch four, out of seven, on a 280-metre (918-foot) route on El Macizo del Pisón, Riglos, Spain. See photo, page 187.

    While Fred and his partner climbed their route, Monique Forestier and I took a companion route that paralleled it to the right: Carnavalada with pitches of 6a+, 6a+, 6a, 7a+,7a, 7a, 6b. Monique acted as my rope run, leading every pitch, which I followed by climbing or using ascenders on the fixed rope that she had also trailed so that I could stop when opportunities arose to shoot Fred. Slowed by some route-finding difficulties near the end, we topped out only to be hit by gale-force winds on top – winds so strong that we could barely stand up. Abseiling off the back of the formation turned into a scary epic, in the dark, nearly hypothermic, struggling to untangle knots in our ropes created by the fierce winds. What could have been one easy abseil to the shelter of the saddle turned into three short ones and a rope management nightmare. We eventually made it down to the base of the cliff at 1 a.m., to be greeted by Fred, who was rather concerned.

BIOGRAPHIES

SIMON CARTER was born in Canberra, Australia, in 1966. As a teenager, Simon developed a fascination for both photography and rock climbing. He completed a Bachelor of Arts in Outdoor Education at La Trobe University, Bendigo, in 1990. Simon began working as a professional photographer and established his business, Onsight Photography and Publishing (www.onsight.com.au), in 1994.

Simon is the author of several other illustrated books, including *Rock Climbing in Australia* and *World Climbing: Rock Odyssey*. His awards include the King Albert Medal of Merit for Achievements in the Mountain World (2000), the Rick White Memorial Medal for Services to and Achievements in Australian Climbing (2009) and the Camera Extreme Laureate awarded by the Explorer's Festival Poland (2010).

Simon lives in the Blue Mountains near Sydney. He works as an outdoors photographer and publisher of rock-climbing guidebooks.

ADAM ONDRA started climbing around the same time he learned to walk. He is now a four-time World Champion in sport climbing and a two-time European Champion (lead climbing). In 2017, when Adam finished his project *Silence* in Norway, he established the hardest route in the world (9c).

STEVE McCLURE is one of the world's leading all-round rock climbers. He has been at the forefront of British sport climbing for over twenty years, with ascents of the country's first 9a+ and 9b. However, he also excels in all areas of rock climbing, including traditional, multi-pitch, bouldering and deep-water solo, and has climbed in locations around the world from South America to Asia, Australia, Africa, Europe, Greenland, the USA and Canada.

GREG CHILD has been climbing for more than half a century. His journey has taken him to cliffs and mountains worldwide, including multi-day big wall ascents in Yosemite and Baffin Island, north of the Arctic Circle, and high-altitude routes such as a successful ascent of K2 in 1990. He is the author of several climbing books and lives in southern Utah.

ALISON OSIUS lives in Western Colorado. Formerly of *Climbing*, *Rock and Ice* and *Ascent* magazines, she now works as a travel editor at *Outside*.

AMITY WARME is a professional rock climber, perpetually seeking the next adventure. She lives in a van with her husband Connor and they spend much of the year travelling to various climbing destinations. Amity is also a sports dietitian.

LIV SANSOZ is a two-time climbing world champion, three-time overall World Cup winner, French national team member and mountain guide with an insatiable appetite for the alpine. She recently knocked off all eighty-two summits above 4,000 metres (13,123 feet) in the Alps in just over a year – skiing and paragliding down to show off.

DAILA OJEDA was born in the Canary Islands. She started climbing when she was eighteen before moving to Catalonia, one of the global epicentres for hard sport climbing. Daila is an active member of the climbing community, sending routes up to 5.14c/8c+, travelling around the globe to share her passion as a professional athlete.

TIM EMMETT is a professional athlete, speaker and coach. He has established many first ascents globally and is a pioneer of deep-water soloing (DWS) and para alpinism (climbing and BASE jumping). Tim enjoys many other sports including skiing, snow boarding, free diving, skeleton, mountain biking and heli boarding.

ACKNOWLEDGMFNTS

My sincerest thanks go to everyone who helped with photo shoots over the years. Some were a lot of work, and not everything went smoothly. Climbers, belayers and others assisted in many ways. Whether it was at the crag or helping us get there, whether it was two or twenty years ago, whether the images made the final selection or not, it was all part of the process that led to the creation of this book.

I really appreciate the inspiration and positivity that so many climbers shared with me, which has been crucial for keeping me going.

There has also been a lot of work behind the scenes. I am very grateful to those who believed in me and sustained my work and business in some way. Naturally, I'm very grateful to my family, friends and colleagues for their support at different times. There are far too many names to mention everyone.

Thank you to the team who saw the concept for this book through to realization, particularly Lucas Dietrich and Helen Fanthorpe at Thames & Hudson, and designer Callin Mackintosh.

I dedicate this book to my daughter, Coco, and her generation. I hope you get the same opportunities, as I have, to explore and experience the world in interesting, meaningful and positive ways.

INDEX

On the front cover: Olivier Michellod climbing *Typhoon* (7c), Telendos Island, Greece
On the back cover: Tony Barron climbing *Agamemnon* (10) at Mount Arapiles, Victoria, Australia

Page 1: Toni Lamprecht on *Manara-Potsiny* (8a) on Tsaranoro Be, Tsaranoro Massif, Madagascar
Page 2: Ashlee Hendy with Elizabeth Chong belaying, *The Man Who Sold the World* (25), the Grampians, Victoria, Australia
Page 4: Ben Heason climbing *Slipstream* (E6, 6b) on Rainbow Slab in the Llanberis Slate Quarries, Wales, UK
Pages 6–7: Leo Houlding at work on *The Northern Celestial Masters* (5.12+), Mount Huashan, China
Pages 10–11: Mike Doyle leading, with Monique Forestier belaying, on the Monkey Face, The Backbone, Smith Rock, Oregon, USA
Pages 16–17: Michael Schön on *Finlandia* (6b), Torre Grande, Cinque Torri in the Dolomites.

The climbing grades cited in the captions correspond to the table on page 241

First published in the United Kingdom in 2024 by
Thames & Hudson Ltd, 181A High Holborn, London WC1V 7QX

First published in the United States of America in 2024 by
Thames & Hudson Inc., 500 Fifth Avenue, New York, New York 10110

The Art of Climbing © 2024 Thames & Hudson Ltd, London
Foreword © 2024 Adam Ondra
Contributor texts © 2024 the respective authors

All photographs by Simon Carter, except page 12: Carter collection; page 13: Ray Vran/Carter collection; page 236 top: Ben Pritchard/Carter collection; page 236 middle: John J O'Brien/Carter collection; page 236 bottom: Lucas Trihey/Carter collection.

Interior layout designed by Callin Mackintosh

British Library Cataloguing-in-Publication Data
A catalogue record for this book is available from the British Library

Library of Congress Control Number 2023948198

ISBN 978-0-500-02597-0

Printed and bound in China by Toppan Leefung Printing Limited

Be the first to know about our new releases, exclusive content and author events by visiting
thamesandhudson.com
thamesandhudsonusa.com
thamesandhudson.com.au